TIGER JOE

A PHOTOGRAPHIC DIARY OF A
WORLD WAR II
AERIAL RECONNAISSANCE PILOT

JOE THOMPSON & TOM DELVAUX

Published by Eveready Press/Jadyn M. Stevens, Editor
Nashville, Tennessee
Book Design by Melissa Solomon
Nashville, Tennessee

Second Printing

ISBN 0-9758714-7-1

ACKNOWLEDGEMENTS

This story of survival in World War II is the measure of support provided by fellow pilots, staff officers, crew chiefs and enlisted personnel. Also, I am grateful to the Royal Air Force and the people of England, Normandy and Belgium.

I want to express my sincere appreciation to the staff of Eveready Press for their enthusiasm, encouragement and final acceptance of this project, and my lasting gratitude to my gifted, faithful scribe, Tom Delvaux, who was persuaded by my daughter Mindy T. Orman to take on this job.

A special thanks to the staff of the Nashville Room of the Nashville Public Library.

Many of Joe Thompson's photos seen here are available:
Joe Thompson, Jr. Papers, Nashville Room, Nashville Public Library

DEDICATION

JT
To my devoted wife, Martha Crook Thompson, and
to my mother, Florence Fondé Thompson

TCD
To my mother, Jean McConnell Delvaux

TABLE OF CONTENTS

PROLOGUE: NOVEMBER 1942

"Basingstoke. Basingstoke. Everyone out for Basingstoke."

The sound of the old conductor's voice singing out the next stop woke me from a fitful half sleep.

I was returning by train from a 3-day pass in London to my duty station, the air base at Middle Wallop, England. Around me, young soldiers, hardly more than boys, sat huddled together, their faces barely visible in the blacked-out railroad car, with only an occasional voice breaking the silence, asking for a cigarette or a piece of chocolate. Some faces gazed out the window at what could be seen of the passing English countryside, illuminated only by the moon, but most of us had turned inward. Lulled by the steady rocking motion of the train and the comforting click-clack of the rails, we tried to doze away the last few minutes of our liberty.

It was a futile attempt, at least for me. Invariably, just as my mind folded itself up into the haze of sleep, the old conductor came trooping through to announce another stop. He was just doing his job, of course, but to me, the sound of those little towns rang like the chimes of a dead man's clock. The further west we traveled away from London, the closer we were to returning to the war.

Decades later, the same men huddled around me, and millions like them, would be called "The Greatest Generation," but at that moment, all I saw were the sons of farmers and carpenters and prayerful mothers on their way to do a job they knew had to be done.

The stop after Basingstoke was mine. Courting sleep, I closed my eyes, hoping the inevitable would never come.

A cold chill came over me. I gathered my things and stepped off the train. Ahead of me was more tough sledding: flying missions, dodging flak and wondering if I would make it through the war, or even enjoy another 3-day pass.

And yet, somehow, I did.

- Joe Thompson

TRAINING DAYS

Our first training plane, the PT-19, lined up on the dusty plains of Hicks Field, Texas.
Incredibly forgiving in the air, it was called the "Cradle of Heroes."

THE CALM BEFORE THE STORM

In the spring of 1941, as a college senior about to graduate from Vanderbilt University, I lived in a world charged with hope and anticipation. Diploma in hand, I felt I had achieved a major milestone, a confirmation, of sorts, that I was now an adult. Everything that had preceded this moment seemed secondary to what now lay ahead: the grand voyage that would be the rest of my life. The future was as yet unwritten; everything seemed possible.

Nature itself seemed caught up in my exuberance. Irrepressible spring brought warmer and warmer days, the bright buds on the trees blooming, the once dormant grass now lush and green. Life abundant, bursting forth. And yet, beneath this vibrant scene, there lay a vague, deep sense of foreboding. We knew the world was in turmoil: Europe in the grip of two madmen, Asia at war now for more than four years. Military service seemed inevitable unless we attended graduate school, but that option was not available to me. I had not been studious and earnest in my studies, and my plans to attend medical school had been seriously derailed by my mediocre performance in chemistry.

My fondness for Vanderbilt coeds determined, in part, my destiny. I wanted to meet the pretty girls that seemed to be everywhere on campus, but having a shy disposition, I knew I needed an ice-breaking technique, one that would give me credible reason to approach an unknown coed and initiate a conversation.

And so I volunteered to be a photographer for the college yearbook. With my camera strapped around my neck, I could walk up to any girl and innocently say, "Would you like to have your picture in the Commodore yearbook?" Who could resist? Thus began my lifelong interest in photography.

My other interest at the time was flying. I had already accumulated 15 hours of flying time in a Piper Cub through my experience with a civilian flying training program completed during my senior year at Vanderbilt.

So when an Air Force recruiter promised an enlistment that combined both my interests, I took the bait. I would first learn to fly, earning my second lieutenant bars in the process. Later, at Randolph Field, I would decide to become an aerial reconnaissance pilot, flying over enemy territory to photograph enemy positions. I had no desire to become a bomber pilot. Flying in formation on a prescribed course with no opportunity to control one's destiny by zigging, zagging and otherwise avoiding enemy fire was not for me. Nor did I find appealing the dramatic and often deadly aerial antics of a combat fighter pilot.

During a six-week period between graduation and my reporting for duty, I worked part-time on the Vanderbilt campus. Then, in August 1941, three buddies and I piled into a Model A my father had bought for $75 and drove cross-county to Hicks Field outside of Fort Worth, Texas. I was 22.

Phi Delta Theta Fraternity, Vanderbilt University, Spring 1941.
I'm on the front row, far right.

HICKS FIELD

On the dry, bare plains of Hicks Field, in what seemed to be an endless succession, stood the first challenge on our way to becoming combat aviators: the PT-19 (*page 1*). Specifically created for training novice pilots by famed aircraft designer Armand Thiebolt, the Fairchild PT-19 Cornell was a single-engine, low-wing plane with two cockpits. It was inexpensive to build, using largely "non-strategic" materials; for example, the wing and tail were sheathed in plywood. In addition, the plane's low wing allowed for a widely spaced fixed landing gear and more secure landings. Incredibly forgiving in the air, the PT-19 was called the "Cradle of Heroes." It was a joy to fly.

There were 30 cadets to a barrack, and for each of us, the next 2 1/2 months became a crucible that tested our talent, knowledge and nerves. There was much to learn and little time to learn it. The pressure was on, and it showed. Indeed, the washout rate at Hicks Field was about 30 percent. I was one of the lucky ones, in part because of my previous flying experience at Vanderbilt.

BEING FOLLOWED BY TIGER JOE

In leaving Nashville and joining the Army, I found myself, for the first time, surrounded by people who did not know me. No one knew any specifics about my past or my family. I enjoyed having this fresh start, but it lasted only a short time.

Letters from home soon arrived, addressed to "Tiger Joe," a nickname bestowed upon me in the summer of my 14th or 15th year. What friends and family had called me at home immediately became my appellation among my soldier colleagues and followed me throughout my military service.

I had acquired the nickname in fighting for a girl whose name I no longer remember. A friend named Dayton Manier and I were boxing at Camp Greenbrier. We were using large heavily padded gloves that made it difficult to inflict any real injury, just two boys clowning around until Dayton made a snide remark about my purported girlfriend.

I had no choice but to defend her honor. He was a heavier and stronger boy than I, but I was more agile and proceeded to pummel him pretty hard. Someone remarked that I fought like a tiger. And so Tiger Joe was born.

My performance on the football field at the time only served to enhance the use of my feline nickname. I was known for my tenacious effort playing in the center of the line —left guard, center, right guard. They said I was a real tiger on the field. More like a scrawny alley cat. I was over six feet tall and weighed a scant 130 pounds, by far the gangliest of the 14 members of the Wallace School football team. Combine that physique with a football jersey emblazoned with the number "1" on the front and back, and the overall effect was that I looked like a thermometer.

"SCATES, A.J."

Our days at Hicks Field (except for Sundays) began precisely at 5:30 a.m. with roll call, a perfunctory ritual held in the pre-dawn darkness. The captain of each unit would call out the name of each cadet, last name first, then the person's first and middle initials. Each captain would then report their findings to the cadet commander, for example, "All present and accounted for, sir."

Roll call was like much of military life—standardized, predictable, and therefore, utterly boring. For the most part, we accepted the strict routines of our new life cheerfully, using humor to interject what levity we could. For example, one morning a captain who talked in a heavy Czechoslovakian accent announced the status of his unit by saying, "What the hell are we doing here, sir?" The cadet commander let it pass. Such instances of minor insubordination, when done in good humor, served to raise morale by giving voice to an otherwise silent yet commonly shared protest. After all, "What the hell were we doing here?" —standing in a dark and dusty field in the middle of Texas?

It was during roll call that I first became familiar with the name "Scates, A.J." Life was always lively when you were around A.J. Scates, a slim, garrulous fellow whose winsome ways allowed him to engage in a series of mishaps and pranks that, for anybody else, would have resulted in serious disciplinary measures.

During one training flight in the two-cockpit PT-19, Scates' instructor pulled back on the throttle and told Scates to prepare for a forced landing, a common training procedure known as a check ride. Scates now had to find a place to land, correctly maneuver the plane into the wind as he descended, and then indicate that he was ready to land by yelling "Flaps" at the correct altitude.

When Scates looked down, he saw they were above a large lake. Still, at an attitude of 5,000 feet, there was plenty of time to find a suitable landing area, but Scates had a different idea. He circled the lake again and again, slowly descending. The instructor said nothing. Then, a mere 15 or so feet above the water, Scates leveled out and instead of the customary "Flaps," he yelled out "Pontoons!" The furious instructor gunned the throttle and took the plane back up to 5,000 feet, where he again pulled back the throttle and announced a forced landing. This time they were over a sizable forest, but a clear area was within easy reach. Undeterred by the anger of his instructor or any possible repercussions, Scates calmly brought the plane down to about 200 feet above the forest and yelled "Timber."

Another incident involving Scates was far more serious. By this time, we were flying the AT-6, an advanced trainer, at Brooks Field in Texas. We soon discovered that our plane's radio could pick up some wildly rhythmic music from a station in Mexico, a welcome reprieve from the instructions issued ceaselessly by the Brooks control tower. We were making practice landings when Scates came in, with his landing gear up. Apparently, Scates was listening to the Mexican radio station, completely oblivious to the frantic screams from the control tower, "Get your landing gear down!" The AT-6 featured a warning system that alerted novice pilots if their landing gear was still up when they slowed the plane, but Scates had the music turned up so loud, he couldn't even hear the blaring horn. He leveled the plane out beautifully, then made a perfect landing on the plane's belly, smashing the propeller and incurring the full fury of his superiors. Amazingly, that was the extent of his punishment. Scates was one of those people who seemed to have been granted a lifetime immunity from punishment by the powers that be. No doubt you've also met the type.

A DAY OF INFAMY—RANDOLPH FIELD

Apparently, our unit scored high marks during our training at Hicks Field, for we soon received advancement to Randolph Field in San Antonio.

Though the two stations were only 170 miles apart, Randolph Field had a much more prestigious pedigree than Hicks. After opening in 1923 as the world's first helium plant, only to be closed six years later because of a shortage of helium, Hicks Field was reactivated in July 1940 for primary flight training, then deactivated in 1945. Randolph Field, which in those days was known as the West Point of the Air, was dedicated on June 30, 1930 as a flying training base and continues with that mission today.

Certain advancements in the military are much like progressing to the next grade in school, for example, from junior high to high school. At first, you are quite proud of your newly acquired status, until you are quickly deflated by the realization that, once again, you are low man on the totem pole.

Such was the case when our unit was assigned to Randolph Field. At the end of our 10 weeks of training at Hicks Field, we ruled the roost as the most experienced cadets on the base. Now the tables were turned. We were underclassmen again, and our new and shiny field blue uniforms did little to compensate for our lessened position.

Although they were just a few months more advanced than we in their training, the upper classmen found plenty of occasions to remind us of our inferior standing. Nothing malicious on their part—just absurdly ludicrous orders. For example, we were greeted one morning by heavy storms, and after marching to breakfast and back through the deluge, an air of relaxation settled in as if we were suddenly on vacation, for we knew there would be no flying in such inclement weather.

That sense of euphoria was short-lived, however, when our upper classmen made their presence known and ordered us to sweep the rain off the ramps in front of the barracks. So there we were, about 100 cadets engaged in the totally futile exercise of sweeping up water in a downpour. I had been exposed to this kind of low-grade intimidation and hazing during my freshman year at Vanderbilt, and I knew that keeping a sense of humor about it all would serve me well.

It was at Randolph Field that we first heard the news of Pearl Harbor.

It was Sunday, our one day off. This was to be the last such Sunday we would enjoy for quite a while. Our training intensified and took on a new urgency that would not permit a weekly day of leisure. Each cadet was also issued seven bullets for our 1907 Springfield rifles. This was done, I was told, in case a Japanese plane, launched from an enemy submarine in the Gulf, attacked our outpost. Our defense would be a fusillade of rifle shots from 500 cadets. Pathetically, that was to be our anti-aircraft battery.

Other than that, not much really changed. For America, the world turned upside down on December 7, but for the squadron of young cadets at Randolph Field, it was only a confirmation of our expectations. We had always known, at least tacitly, that all this intensive training was not undertaken so we could simply serve in a peacetime Army.

The war was on now. And we were knee-deep in it.

SEARCHING FOR THE GREEN LIGHT

Charles Lindbergh graduated from my next training destination: the Primary Flying School at Brooks Field, also near San Antonio. Here, as my flying skills developed and improved, I gained greater confidence in the air. Going up on a clear day, looking down upon the earth below, stretched out beneath the sky, I felt as if a beautiful kingdom was mine to behold. The smallness of everything—the cars, the buildings, the people, the Texas hills—from such a height gave the scene a charming, doll-house quality, as if the earth and all it contained was but the setting of some long-forgotten fairy tale.

This sense of the make-believe, as well as my newly gained confidence, were soon to disappear, however, for I was shortly to come face to face with the reality, and the danger, of flying at night.

Our night-flying training commenced with a simple enough exercise. We took off, alone in our training plane, then leveled off and circled the field at a prescribed altitude, say 2,000 feet. The tower would call our number to land on the lighted airstrip. After touching down, we would take off again and repeat the procedure.

But on this night, the training exercise was to be far more challenging. For the first time, we were to fly cross-country on a specific heading, identify some landmarks on the route (marked by a large well-lit letter), then turn around on a reverse heading for home. Blinking lights set up along the route would help us confirm our position.

It all seemed reasonably simple—until the weather changed and a wall of ragged low-hanging clouds called scud blew in. Needless to say, it's not the kind of weather you want for your first cross-country night flight.

My plane was one of the last five to leave before they scrubbed the mission because of the advancing weather. I never got the word to return to base because my radio was on the blink. As I flew on, oblivious to the situation, I took out my map to confirm the location of a landmark, but a slight crack in the fuselage had created a wind tunnel, and the map flew out of my hand into the back seat, out of my reach. Then I saw the scud. Soon I would be flying blind, without a map.

I knew I had to do something so I decided to duck down below the clouds. I went lower and lower until I broke through the cloudbank and could see cars on the road, where unsuspecting drivers had no idea of the trouble I was in.

I was in trouble, and I knew it. Then I remembered a passing remark by an instructor that easily could have gone unnoticed, but somehow had stuck with me. He had told us there were two light lines leading back to San Antonio. Each light was about five miles apart and had a blinking signal. If I could just find one of these light lines, I could follow it all the way home. So I turned my plane around, still flying low, and headed on the bearing for San Antonio, feeling somewhat relieved about my situation until I checked my gas gauge. It was precariously low. Apparently, I had been flying around aimlessly for longer than I supposed. But here again, I remembered a piece of information that the instructor had mentioned. Along both of the light lines were a number of emergency landing fields, each indicated by a blinking green light.

So I began to look for the green light in earnest. And in just a few moments, I saw it: a single spot of green, winking at me out of the immensity of the night sky. I felt the joy of a child lost in the woods, who suddenly glimpses the lights of his house and knows that he is safely home.

With salvation so near, I wasn't about to take any chances. I circled the airstrip three times just to make sure it was clear. I put down my wheels, lowered the flaps and put her down, coming to a stop with about 20 yards of runway to spare.

The solid earth felt like heaven. I taxied to the center of the runway and noticed a small building from which emerged an old Texas farmer wearing bib overalls. He was as surprised to see me as I was glad to see him. I told him I needed to use his telephone to call Brooks Field and make them aware of my situation. I was expecting to be severely chastised by my training officers, but instead they were glad to hear from me and highly complimentary of my actions.

I found out later that two other pilots didn't make it back that night, victims of the scud. And so I learned the importance of keeping cool in a tight situation and using your head.

THE COLONEL'S ADMONITION

In March 1942, my parents traveled from Nashville to San Antonio to attend my graduation at Brooks Field, where I was to receive my commission as a second lieutenant.

In hindsight, I wish they hadn't made the long journey. For by attending, their general anxiety about what the future held for me was transformed into an acute and vivid distress by the callous comments of a full-bird Colonel. After making a few preparatory remarks to the newly minted officers, the colonel laid bare the stark and brutal future that awaited us.

"Second lieutenants," he declared. "Look at the man to your left."
He paused dramatically as we complied.

"Now look at the man to your right."
Another pause.

"A year from now," he announced with the certainty of a scientific fact, "one of the three of you will be dead, and the other two will be Captains!"
And that was that.

The colonel, I believe, uttered his unflinching statement as a call to arms and a preparation for battle, and his pithy illustration did hit home. But what he said horrified my parents and, in retrospect, seemed cruelly unnecessary.

Because I had requested photographic reconnaissance, I was to stay on at Brooks Field for another month or so, flying the O-52, an ancient aircraft built in the mid-1920s. It was all our government had to offer, while across the Atlantic the Germans, for almost a decade, had been churning out increasingly superior aircraft in greater and greater volumes. Even today, that disparity re-ignites my anger over the lack of understanding, exhibited by our political leaders in the years leading up to Pearl Harbor, concerning the rise of Nazi Germany and Imperial Japan.

My next assignment was with the 30th Observation Squadron in Atlanta, where the planes were equally antiquated. In particular, there was the O-47, no more than a Sunday afternoon cruiser designed for duty in the National Guard, and similar to the O-52. You could always tell an O-52 pilot because, like the tennis pro Rod Laver, his left arm was twice as big as his right. That's because the O-52 required the pilot to pump the wheels down and lock them by hand—52 pumps, we claimed. Such was the state of our military in 1942.

The 30th Observation Squadron, which was to become the 109th Tactical Squadron, was ill equipped and under staffed. This was to be my overseas squadron, but as is often the case with the military, everything changed when the powers that be suddenly decided there was a greater need for twin-engine pilots. We were given co-pilot training in the B-25 "Mitchell," named after the famous pioneer of military aviation, General Billy Mitchell, and used by General Doolittle in his famous Tokyo Raid, which took place at about this time, on April 18, 1942.

After only seven hours of this co-pilot training, I found myself on the end of a runway, seated alone in a twin-engine A-20 and preparing for take-off. Such hurried training had become a matter of course now that the war was raging on several fronts. Indeed, after only two months of training with the twin-engine aircraft, the Army Air Force again re-shifted its priorities, and I was flying single-engine aircraft again. By the time I was shipped overseas to the European Theater in October 1942, I had a mere 15 hours of total flying time in the P-40 and the P-51A with the Allison engine, which served as my combat plane. In later months, replacement pilots sent to my squadron would have 150 hours. But soon, I was to receive my training from the world's most experienced authority, the elite fighter pilots of the Royal Air Force.

AN AMERICAN IN ENGLAND

Our unit on assignment in Wales, where we practiced calling in artillery
adjustments from the air.

THE BIG APPLE SNAFU

You could feel it in the air: a pervasive and heightened sense of anticipation. Snippets of overheard conversations and countless rumors, careening rapidly from person to person, fueled the expectant mood. The subject was always the same: when would we be leaving the country and, most importantly, to what combat area would we be assigned? Details were sketchy, but we knew that our departure was imminent.

Only a few days before we shipped out from Atlanta, I learned that we would be leaving for England from New York City. I was able to inform my parents, who made a special effort to come and see me off in the Big Apple. But just like their journey to San Antonio, their trip resulted in unexpected distress.

A train transported us from Atlanta to New Jersey, where we were temporarily housed at an Army base. Almost immediately, our superiors asked for volunteers to serve as an advance party and board the ship that would take us overseas. For reasons unknown to me, perhaps because our barracks were so dismal or perhaps because I wanted to fulfill my duty as a resident of the Volunteer State, I offered my services. That turned out to be my undoing, for no one had informed me that once you boarded the ship, you were not permitted to go back ashore. Why this rule was in effect, I have no idea. Meanwhile, back on shore, my landlubber buddies were granted a 3-day pass to see the sights of the Big Apple. You can imagine my jealousy and frustration.

Worse yet, I was unable to contact my parents, who had arrived in New York City and stayed for a week, waiting for me to contact them, then assuming I had already shipped out. And so there were no teary good-byes. Perhaps that was for the best, especially for my mother.

On September 27, 1942, we sailed from New York aboard a former Dutch luxury cruiser, filled to capacity as a troop transport. My fellow officers and I did enjoy some perks. We ate three times a day in a fine dining room, where we shared company with some female American nurses. But that was little compensation when we stepped out at night onto the blacked-out deck, with all the boats in the convoy moving like dim shadows across a silent sea, occasionally interrupted by the lonely wail of a siren warning us of an approaching U-boat. We lost one small boat, carrying cargo, in the convoy. Not until we rounded the Firth of Clyde and landed in Glasgow did we know we were safe. By early October, I arrived at the Membury Airdrome in Berkshire, England. Only 13 months earlier, I had been an eager young cadet on the brown dusty plains of Fort Worth. Now I was in verdant England, ready to win the war single-handedly. But real combat and actual missions would have to wait, giving me time to explore this welcoming country and my newfound home.

FLYING BACK IN TIME

Within a few days of our arrival in England, we were back in the air, but not to continue our combat training. We had no planes available for that. However, in order to log the four hours of flying time required each month to earn our extra flying pay, we were given the opportunity to fly a legend of the air, the Tiger Moth. A descendant of the Gipsy Moth, the Tiger Moth looked like something out of World War I. This open-cockpit single-engine bi-plane became one of the world's most famous training aircraft and provided the majority of the RAF pilots with their first flying experience. The Tiger Moth was easy to fly, but in many respects it was technologically primitive. For example, there was no air speed indicator on the dash; instead, a small plank with a pointer, located on the wing, indicated air speed when preparing to land.

I will never forget my first view of the British countryside from the air. Compared to a plane with a closed cockpit, flying in an open-cockpit creates a much more tangible and intimate connection with the surrounding earth and sky. In much the same way, riding on a motorcycle or in a convertible gives you the feeling that the countryside is waiting to embrace you with open arms.

The ceiling was low that day, about 500 feet. Looking like a World War I ace with my goggles on (all that was lacking was a long, elegant scarf blowing in the wind), I dipped the plane down below the clouds and beheld a green and magical landscape. There was a village so quaint and rustic, it seemed to be inhabited by serfs, and a tiny, Norman-style church, straight from the 14th century. A long row of ancient trees hugged the earth high on a hill, and nearby, there stood the manor house, where I imagined a duke and his duchess held court. I was fascinated and delighted with this new country.

Finally, thanks to a reverse Lend-Lease agreement, we were able to obtain some old MK 5 Spitfires for training purposes. These gallant planes were the lucky few that had survived the Battle of Britain, and they had seen their better days. But they would do for the time, and the hours spent flying these venerable Spitfires would serve me well when I was sent to Cornwall to train with the RAF.

The English called them Land Army Girls—women who worked the fields to replace the farmers now turned soldiers.

THE FEW

"Never in the field of human conflict was so much owed by so many to so few."

So Winston Churchill expressed his admiration and gratitude to the pilots of the RAF. At a time when Britain stood alone against the Nazi war machine, the RAF was the only line of defense between Hitler and the complete subjugation of Europe.

In July 1940, the Germans, fresh off their conquest of France, turned their sights on the invasion of Britain, which was given the code name Sea Lion. Before the proposed assault of 160,000 German soldiers could take place, Hitler's generals wanted to destroy the Royal Air Force and win air superiority over the English Channel.

The Luftwaffe stationed 2,800 aircraft in France, outnumbering the RAF four to one. The English did have one advantage: the German fighters could only stay in England's air space for about half an hour before low fuel forced them to return to their home bases. The attacks began on July 10, 1940 with the Luftwaffe assaulting convoys in the English Channel as well as ports and radar stations on the south coast.

At the beginning of August, the fighting intensified. From August 1 – 18, the RAF lost 208 fighters and 106 pilots. Soon, the loss of planes and pilots outstripped the production of new aircraft and the training of pilots to fly them.

Just when the RAF was nearing its breaking point, the Germans made a costly mistake: accidentally bombing a civilian section of London. Hitler had banned such attacks, hoping for a negotiated peace. In retaliation, the Brits launched a successful bombing attack on Berlin that incensed Hitler, who then changed the Lufwaffe's objective from military to civilian targets. The Blitz was on.

The Germans hoped such attacks on London would break the morale of the English people, but it only stiffened it. The new tactic also enabled the RAF to regain its strength and rebuild its airfields and defenses.

Slowly, the Germans gave up on defeating the RAF. Winter was approaching, the weather was deteriorating. Operation Sea Lion was cancelled. Hitler turned his attention to the invasion of Russia. Britain was, for the moment, safe and free.

Of the 2,353 men from Great Britain and 574 from overseas who participated as pilots and other aircrew during the Battle of Britain from July 10 to October 31, 1940, 544 lost their lives. Another 791 were killed later in the war.

Now I would have the opportunity to fly with those men who had survived. My assignment was in Perranporth, Cornwall, a hard place to find, it turned out, for all the road signs had been removed in case the Germans invaded and needed directions. The corporal who was driving got all turned around, but eventually we arrived in a beautiful little seaside port with a wide mile-long beach.

We had to land our planes on a little air strip flying right into the face of a 400-foot cliff overlooking the beach, with the air thermals and wind gusts buffeting the plane. That took some doing.

When I arrived in Britain, I was in no way ready for combat. Flying with the RAF changed all that. I was learning from pilots who had survived the Battle of Britain, who had not "gone to the well once too often," as was said with typical British understatement. Nonchalant, unassuming, yet fiercely dedicated to their mission, they taught me how to fly. They got me ready to go to war, instead of merely posing for it.

The Few—Members of the 66th Squadron, my RAF unit. Andrew Deytrikh is standing second from right.

STRIKING A POSE

I didn't think I would make it through the war, so I had this picture taken as a kind of official portrait to send to my mother.

I wanted to look my best, of course. Looking back now, however, the whole thing seems stilted and posed. It's really a picture of a scared kid, trying his best to look like a brave soldier.

The scarf around my neck, for example, is something I must have picked up from the movies. The crush hat I'm wearing supposedly signifies that the wearer has flown 50 combat missions, though when the picture was taken I had yet to see combat. I'm wearing a custom-made Eisenhower jacket because, well, that was the thing to wear. Amazingly, it still fits today. And then there are the official RAF boots, which I obtained in a trade with an English pilot. This was footwear that could save your life. There was a little knife tucked in one of the uppers. If you happened to be shot down over France, you could use the knife to cut off the tops of the boots and create your basic civilian shoe. So the Germans, at least at first glance, wouldn't suspect you were an enemy pilot. It was all very ingenious and very British in its attention to detail.

I'm standing in front of a P-51 Mustang. The plane I flew for several months, when I was attached to the Royal Air Force (66th Squadron), was a Mark V Spitfire. Look closely and you'll see a tiny RAF button in my blouse. I traded my American button for it so everyone would be sure to know I had flown with the RAF.

(R) The Spitfire was a very light plane and tended to float. The pilot of this plane was accustomed to landing on American runways that were twice as long as the ones we used overseas. When he realized he had used up too much runway, he jammed on the brakes, and the plane's nose dove into the ground.

FLYING WITH THE RAF

During my six or seven weeks with the 66th RAF Squadron at Perranporth, I had the opportunity, if that's the word, to fly combat missions. Usually, our assignment involved providing cover for B-25s and other bombers, whose target was often the Nazi submarine pens located along the Brest Peninsula in northwest France.

Our squadron of Spitfires would fly across the English Channel above the bombers at about 12,000 feet. From that position, we could dive down and gain valuable speed to catch and surprise the German fighters when we spotted them advancing upward to intercept the bombers.

The right timing was imperative. An experienced and knowledgeable squadron commander knew exactly when to descend from the heights: too soon and the Germans would disengage; too late put the bombers in peril. We usually dove down in three flight lines, four planes to a flight. I soon realized that, being the green American, they always put me in the top flight, the last to go down, so I would have the help and assistance of the flights preceding me. My flight leader, a fellow named Andrew Deytrikh, later acknowledged that he gave me this position. It probably saved my neck.

What is hard to convey totally, at least with words, is the sense of immense space that envelopes you up there, among the clouds, surrounded in sound by the steady snarling roar of the Spitfire's Rolls Royce Merlin engine.

Once, coming back from a mission over the Brest Peninsula, we encountered a problem. A thick blanket of cloud cover, beginning at the water's edge, had settled in from 500 to a 1,000 feet. We had two choices: either fly back out and come in under the clouds at 500 feet or conduct a standard instrument landing.

Our CO chose neither. Instead, when he spotted a small opening in the cloud bank, he decided to give it a go, hoping, I suppose, to add a little extra excitement to cap off the day. He gave us the signal to peel off and follow him.

What proceeded was an aerial version of crack the whip, a now-forgotten game of my youth, in which six or eight or ten boys would ice skate holding hands. The leader would skate like a crazy man—curving here, there and yonder—building up the centrifugal force until the last one in line (the caboose) would have to let loose and went flying out of control.

So down we went, 11 Spitfires peeling off behind the CO, I being number 8, each pilot in line having to make a harder and harder turn to follow the leader through this ever tightening hole, not knowing when we could pull up below the clouds, all the time gathering speed, with the blood rushing out of your head so your vision turned dull and then grey, and you had to fight to pull your neck back and breathe to keep the oxygen in your brain and yourself alive, until you came out of the clouds just above the trees at 400 mph.

We made it, coming down a mere five miles from the air strip. The excitement wasn't over, however. For now we were to land using a technique designed to get us on the ground in a hurry in case the German fighters followed us back. Four planes landed right behind each other, each turning off the runway to make room for the next, with about 10 seconds between each touch down.

I was flying with the best. I'll never forget those days.

Andrew Deytrikh, flight leader of the 66th Squadron, my RAF unit. His parents were Russian, but Deytrikh was very British.

"BOGIES AT TWO O'CLOCK"

When my tour of duty ended with the RAF, I returned to Middle Wallop, where I was soon promoted to assistant operations officer. By now, our P-51s were starting to arrive from America, and we began flying air reconnaissance in both the Spitfire and the P-51.

In the spring of '44, with the invasion of France approaching, our missions often involved photographing the French coastline from Cape Grand Nez to Normandy. Because we were using a lateral camera, with its 10-inch lens aimed out the side of the plane at an angle parallel to the ground, we were required to fly at an altitude of only 50 feet in order to photograph the German gun implacements.

During one mission over Abbeville, France, as we approached our target, an urgent call crackled over the radio, "Bogies at two o'clock." Some 4,000 to 5,000 feet above us, we saw what we thought were four FW-190s, the German's most feared fighter plane. We knew that the famous FW-190 Yellow Nose squadron was stationed nearby, and we had no desire to engage these superior planes. Armed with 20 mm guns and nicknamed the "Butcher Bird," the FW-190 was 20 - 35 mph faster at all altitudes, had better acceleration, and could climb steeper and dive faster than the Spitfire, which we were flying that day. Our only advantage was our tighter turning radius.

Guided by our motto, "He who flies and runs away, lives to fly another day," we high tailed it out of there and headed for the coast at maximum throttle. All except our #4, Hogan Jones. Hogan was a gruff, cigar-chomping, curse-word wielding character, a fairly good pilot, but also the butt of many jokes. For some reason, Hogan's plane always seemed slower than the rest of us. I glanced back and saw the planes for the first time in clear silhouette. To my relief, I realized the FW-190s were actually British Typhoons. Then suddenly, even though we were required to maintain radio silence, we heard Hogan Jones pleading, "Hey fellows, wait for me!" He would never live it down. For the next few months a resounding chorus of "Hey fellows, wait for me!" would greet Hogan when he entered the mess hall.

Whenever we arrived back safely, many of the pilots would scurry to the barracks to continue one of their favorite pastimes, reading the Saturday Evening Post. The magazine was running an ongoing serial called "Fair Stood the Wind for France." The story concerned a medium-size bomber that was shot down and the efforts of the crew to return home with the help of the French underground. I suppose their eager interest in the article might be attributed to this simple truth: nothing makes for a better read than a story in which it's easy to imagine yourself, a story that could be describing your next mission.

A long-nosed FW-190, the German fighter plane we most feared.

ENGLISH GIRLS AND HIGH TEA

In February 1943, I received a five-day pass and made the journey by train to Edinburgh and then to Glasgow to see a dear friend for the first time. Her name was Margaret Ruffel. We had corresponded for two years during my college days, and I had continued to write her during flying school. Now that I had the opportunity to see her in person, I wanted to take advantage of it.

I'm glad I did. Margaret turned out to be a strikingly beautiful brunette. She lived in a small, mediocre flat on a very modest income with her widowed mother. But their lack of financial resources, combined with the scarcity of goods due to rationing, did not deter them from being hospitable hosts. That night, they served up a hearty dinner, and the next morning for breakfast, they served me two eggs, soft boiled, their ration for the entire month.

So there we were, a Tennessee boy and an English girl, walking along the banks of Loch Lomond, talking about, of all things, the religious beliefs of the Mormons. Apparently, an enterprising young missionary had spent his mandatory two-year tour in the area and had persuaded Margaret's mother to convert. But now she had some misgivings and wanted to discuss it with an American, thinking perhaps that Utah and Tennessee were in close proximity. With my Presbyterian roots, however, I knew as little about the subject as she did.

Upon returning to Membury, I had the opportunity to experience that quaint English domestic ritual known as high tea. Near the base stood a manor house called Inholmes, home of the Barwick family. Madame Barwick, the lady of the house, invited some American officers over for afternoon tea. We arrived, properly attired in our dress uniforms and were greeted at the front door by a butler, who was exempt from military service because of his wooden leg. He escorted us into a beautiful room where Madame Barwick held court. Before us, on a large table, a number of delightful dishes and appetizing finger foods beckoned to us, a far cry from our usual fare of C-rations. We were ready to chow down, watching our manners, of course, but first there would be the usual polite conversation. After five minutes of amiable chatter, a young lady suddenly entered the room. We rose and greeted Eleanor, Madame Barwick's oldest daughter. Five minutes more of polite conversation and then a second daughter made her entrance. We stood and greeted Diana in the same fashion. Five minutes more and, like clockwork, a third daughter appeared, whose name escapes me. We each began to wonder silently to ourselves how many more daughters would appear. But that was it. Lady Barwick had achieved her mission with regal precision: introducing her three daughters to an entire squad of eligible American officers.

In my office at Middle Wallop, surrounded by my American girlfriends, many of whom wrote me "Dear Joe" letters.

IN THE BLINK OF AN EYE

During the early days of our preparation for the invasion of Europe, I attended an Aircraft Recognition School at Eastbourne. Located just west of Dover, atop the marvelous white cliffs that buttress the English side of the Channel, Eastbourne had the misfortune of being chosen by the Luftwaffe as a training target for its pilots. German fighters routinely zoomed in at a low altitude, dropped their armaments and roared back across the Channel with no chance of being intercepted. These sudden raids could happen at any time, so our time there was quite stimulating.

For several hours each day, RAF teachers instructed us in the methods of quickly identifying any aircraft we might encounter, both friend and foe, which amounted to several dozen aircraft. Our class consisted of American and British officers, as well as two Polish pilots. (The RAF had quite an international roster, with pilots from Poland, Czechoslovakia, New Zealand, Canada, Belgium, Australia, South Africa, France, Ireland, and America, plus one pilot each from Jamaica, South Rhodesia and, of all places, Palestine.)

Once we had mastered this skill, our job was to return to our units and likewise train them, using a projector and a set of flash cards that featured dozens of planes in silhouette. The objective was to identify the plane from the silhouette, which appeared for a mere 1/15th of a second (literally, the blink of an eye).

Our squadron became fairly efficient in this task, highly motivated by the awareness that their newly acquired skill might possibly save their lives.

Such quick recognition was especially vital for air reconnaissance pilots, for unlike larger fighter squadrons, we flew in tandem and therefore had only two sets of eyes to spot enemy aircraft before they spotted us.

For our evening's entertainment, we would gather at a local pub to savor pints of mild British beer. To simplify the drink-ordering process, each pilot would serve as a host and buy a round for the entire table. Once these were imbibed, a new host was designated to buy a new round, and so the night progressed. The pub closed at 10 p.m., and precisely seven minutes before that final hour, the lady bartender would announce "Time, gentlemen, time," the British equivalent of "last call for alcohol." At this point, we usually realized that one or two or our companions had not fulfilled their obligation by serving as host. This was not to be tolerated. So we would rush up to the bar, order one or two pints to collect the outstanding debt, and drink it all in the few minutes that remained. Which explains why, once we negotiated the blacked-out streets of Eastbourne and found our way back to our hotel, we were more than ready for a deep night's sleep.

Members of my unit, the 109th Tactical Reconnaissance Squadron, 9th Air Force.

THREE O' CLOCK IN THE MORNING

I have always been able to sleep, to nod off at a moment's notice and take catnaps in the most unlikely places and circumstances. So when night fell, and my three companions and I settled in our cramped, tiny quarters, I found it easy to forget the day's cares. The instant my head hit the pillow, the deep arms of sleep embraced me and gave me rest.

We welcomed sleep, for it was only then that we found a temporary respite from the low-grade anxiety that was otherwise our constant companion. It was always with us, down in our gut, lingering beneath our off-duty banter and camaraderie, though we never spoke of it directly. We all knew the percentages and updated them precisely as new data arrived. We knew what we were facing. Talking about it would only interfere with keeping our mettle.

And yet, even in the sanctuary of sleep, you were never completely safe. Sometimes at three o' clock in the morning, a sergeant would enter with orders to wake one man for a special mission. This time, it was my turn. The sergeant gently shook me so as not to wake the other men and then whispered in my ear, "Thompson, you take off at four."

It was at that moment, with my mind first gathering itself into alertness, but before the comforting rituals of flight preparation had commenced, that the fear struck deepest. In this unguarded moment, with my bunkmates still succumbed to blissful sleep, I felt totally alone.

This cold fear in the pit of my stomach remained as I dressed in the dark and walked to the flight line. In the blackout conditions, I first heard the engine warming up and then saw the crew chief and the armament men and the radio operator and the photography man loading the film in the camera, all going about their duties, which, when completed, would leave them safely on the ground.

Then my #2 man and I were ready to take off into the blackness, climbing up on the assigned compass heading and, in the now dim light, seeing the edge of the channel and Portland Bill, a prominence just west of Bournemouth. By now, our fear, like football pre-game jitters, had settled down. The game was on. The task at hand would occupy our minds. Time to set another compass heading that took us to the coast of France, east of the Seine River. The light of a new day was breaking now as we crossed into France and began photographing troop movements in Normandy. Then back to the beaches, crossing the channel to our green island home, and, with the wheels of the plane touching down, knowing we were safe, wonderfully safe.

MY COUSIN, THE GENERAL

Like clockwork, on every third day during my stay overseas, I received a letter from my mother, who informed me about the various goings-on of family in specific and Nashville in general. Often in her correspondence, Mother would inquire if I had been able to see my cousin Maxwell, and if I hadn't, wouldn't I please do so for her sake.

Cousin Maxwell was not just another Allied soldier. He was General Maxwell Andrews, a native of Nashville, and one of the most important figures of World War II, although today he is almost entirely forgotten.

Andrews was a pioneer in military aviation, taking the baton from the "Father of the Air Force," the disgraced and court-martialed Billy Mitchell, and overseeing the first independent air wing of the Army. In the fall of 1942, he became commander of all U.S. Forces in the Middle East, establishing the Ninth Air Force during his tenure in Cairo. Early in 1943, Andrews replaced Eisenhower as commander of all American troops in the European Theater. From his headquarters in London, he directed both the American air campaign against Germany and the planning for the ground invasion of Western Europe.

To my mother, however, he was simply Cousin Maxwell. Even though it would require a genealogist to determine if we were second, third or fourth cousins, he was still family, and it was my duty, in my mother's strong opinion, to pay him my respects.

In April 1943, on leave in London, I managed to gather up enough resolve to go and greet my cousin, the General. I found his office, tucked away on one of those tidy little London side streets.

I entered a reception area, nervously told the secretary the purpose of my visit, and waited for several minutes in an agitated state until I was told I could now see the highest ranking American officer in the European Theater.

With as much military dignity as I could muster, I entered the general's office and gave a snappy salute. He stood up from behind his desk, walked over to me, extended his hand, put his arm around my shoulder and said, "Joe, come sit down and tell me about the Belle Meade Country Club."

I felt immediately at ease. We talked about family and Nashville for several minutes, and then I asked for his opinion about a major point of discussion among the GIs: Would the Allies superior air power be able to bomb the Germans into submission and render a land invasion of the Continent unnecessary? General Andrews quickly dismissed the conjecture. Air power alone would not win the war. Not only would an invasion be required, we would also have to fight our way through Europe all the way to Berlin, and that would be a very tough road.

His prediction proved to be correct, but General Maxwell Andrews did not live to see it come true. Three weeks after my visit, on May 3, 1944, he was killed when his B-24 Liberator crashed trying to land in Iceland during bad weather, fulfilling his wish not to be "one of those generals who die in bed." At the time, he was the highest-ranking Allied officer to die in the line of duty during the war.

JENNY

The shafts of light streaming through the railway station begged to be photographed. Looking through my camera's viewfinder, I decided I needed a human figure to add some interest. So I asked my companion, Jenny Staten, to walk though the scene.

I met Jenny when one of our squadron members suffered an eye injury, and I went to visit him at a hospital where Jenny was serving as a nurse. She was an American from upstate New York, and we hit it off immediately.

One day in late May 1944, she called me and said she wanted to see me immediately even though we were hundreds of miles away. Her voice was urgent, and inviting. As a squadron commander, I told my sergeant that I needed to "borrow" a little single-engine Piper-Club-type plane that we used to transport film to headquarters. It was that simple in those days, and I flew down to see Jenny.

Jenny wanted to see me because she knew that the D-Day invasion was imminent, and none of us knew what would happen after that.

D-Day came and went, and the war droned on. Soon I was in Europe and Jenny was stationed at a large hospital in France. Seeing each other became more difficult.

Six months after our pre D-Day rendezvous, somewhere between Belgium and Bastogne, I received a letter from her, informing me that she had met a young doctor at a hospital in France.

I thought that would be the last I would ever hear of Jenny Staten, but I was wrong.

For the first few months after returning home from the war, I found myself depressed and lethargic. When the church bells tolled in Nashville to celebrate VJ-Day, I cared not. All I wanted to do was cut the grass and wander in the fields at home and try to forget the past. Six-feet-four, I had dropped to a mere 140 lbs.

Then I received another letter from Jenny. She was writing to tell me she hadn't married the doctor. She had recently discovered that she couldn't have children and didn't think it fair, given this new information, to hold the doctor to any obligation. Now she was back home in upstate New York and wanted to know if I would come and visit.

I never considered the idea. I had been through enough. I never wrote her back.

ON TO EUROPE

The palace of Versailles, just outside of Paris.

D-DAY MINUS 2

Things really began heating up in the months leading up to June 6, 1944 as men and material streamed into England. A more serious and earnest atmosphere settled in. We all knew something was up.

For weeks now, our missions had involved photographing the northern coast of France as well as documenting German positions as far inland as Paris. We never knew the exact date of the invasion, or where it would occur. So when my #2 and I took off on June 4, we had no idea that the invasion of Normandy would commence in two days.

We had a solid overcast at 3,500 feet that day as we flew past the coast at Bournemouth and crossed the channel, skimming the water at 50 feet. Landfall occurred a bit northeast of Le Havre. We had only encountered very light flak so far, a good sign. The sullen skies were lower now, but below us, the French countryside was deceptively peaceful, dappled green with forests and fields.

Our first mission called for us to photograph a No-Ball target-launching platform for the V-1. The Jerries always built the platforms for these pilotless flying bombs inside a wooded area, and the runway had the rough J-shape of a hockey stick, with the handle pointed toward London.

Our next targets were the airdromes at Evereux, Conches and Dreux. Just a few months earlier, these air bases were the proud home for squadrons of the feared FW-190. But today, the bases seemed almost deserted. Indeed, during our entire mission, we observed no rail traffic, no troop transports, no tank movements. All was quiet, eerily quiet. From Vire in central Normandy, we headed to our final target, Grand Camp, a prominence on the Normandy coast not far from Bayeux. I got the photo. "Everything was in the kitchen," as our RAF colleagues had taught us to say, just 180 miles of Channel water to cross, and we were home safe.

As soon as I rolled to a stop, a young soldier screeched up next to my plane in a jeep. With the propeller blades still turning, he removed the film from the camera and then sped away to deliver the film to Eisenhower's headquarters at Wilton House in Salisbury, some 20 miles away. Two days later I learned why he was in such a hurry: the last target on our mission was a German battery that overlooked a small sandy shore now known forever as Omaha Beach.

On the morning of June 6, 1944, our unit heard about the D-Day invasion.

I took this picture of Omaha Beach about two weeks after D-Day. Those are landing craft bunched together on the shore. On the far right is a floating bridge for vehicles.

D-DAY AND BEYOND

The night before D-Day, the headquarters of the 9th Air Force issued orders for a white stripe to be painted down the center of each aircraft's wings. These markings were to ensure there would be no confusion as to who was friend and who was foe, at least in the air, during the invasion.

It is difficult to describe the scope and magnitude of the naval procession that stretched out beneath us on that sixth day of June: 900 warships and almost 4,100 other craft, everything from ocean liners to fishing boats, stretched out from Bournemouth to Normandy. Indeed, what we beheld was nothing less than the largest armada the world had ever seen, assembled for the specific purpose of launching this greatest military invasion.

We had some planes go down that day, mostly due to bad weather, a few due to German flak, and at least one by friendly fire, despite the white markings. With its square cut shape and bulky front end, the Mustang somewhat resembled a number of German planes, and in the midst of the heightened anxiety and chaos of the day, no doubt many of our naval AA gunners had twitchy trigger fingers.

The plane hit the ocean almost immediately, but the pilot, Lieutenant Keller, quickly exited the wreckage and used his Mae West to stay afloat until a destroyer came over and dropped him a rope ladder. With some difficulty Keller climbed aboard. The skipper of the destroyer immediately greeted him with a bottle of whiskey in one hand and a Purple Heart in the other, telling him how sorry he was that his boys had shot down an American plane.

Lieutenant Keller was back with our squadron in 10 days. More adventures awaited him. In the last week of the war, on his 75th mission, he was shot down over the Rhine Valley and landed on the German side of a tank battle. We assumed he was either KIA or a POW. Then, about a week later, Keller walked into our squadron headquarters at Kassel, looking as if he had just gone out for a long stroll, except for the fact that he was a bit thinner. His prison guards had abandoned their posts, and he had simply walked west to his freedom, asking soldiers along the way where he could find the 109th Squadron.

Lt. Detlef J. Keller from Ogallala, Nebraska. When he was shot down by an American destroyer during the D-Day invasion, the skipper of the offending ship gave him a Purple Heart and a bottle of whiskey along with his apologies.

MY 25TH BIRTHDAY

This picture was taken on June 8, 1944—my 25th birthday The day began at 3:00 a.m. with a shake of my shoulder by an intelligence officer who didn't know and didn't care that it was my birthday! They needed me on a mission. No prior knowledge of the target. Ten minutes to memorize the map, then fly over France.

When I returned, the lack of sleep, combined with the usual strain of flying a mission, left me physically and mentally exhausted. Fifty yards from the air strip I lay down in the grass and went to sleep, joined by a dog, one of our squadron's mascots. Some buddies of mine sneaked up on me, borrowed my camera and took this picture. They took great delight in documenting my apparent slacking off. I was only irritated by their wasting my film to take such a picture. Film was very hard to obtain. Later on, at about two in the afternoon, as I still slumbered in the grass, an Intelligence Officer came over and woke me.

"Thompson," he said, " We've got another mission for you to fly. We need …" and then proceeded to list the various objectives of the mission.

"Wait a minute," I said. "I was just over there at 3:30 this morning."

But that didn't stop him. He just kept telling me what we needed photographed—a bridge here, a road there. And so I found myself heading out for a second mission of the day and thinking to myself, "This is a heck of a way to spend my 25th birthday."

Bulgey Dotterer (left) and Clarence Louden about to leave on a mission. Bulgey stayed in the service and fought in Korea. Clarence was the best poker player in the unit and used his winnings to buy a town lot back home. He had a little dimple in his chin that wiggled when he had a good hand. At least, that's what he told us.

IKE AND THE BRITISH BULLDOG

With the Normandy beachhead secured, the Allied forces pushed deeper into the French countryside as June turned to July. At some point, when our lines reached far enough inland, it made logistical sense to build an airstrip. Located near Le Molay, only five miles from the German lines, it was called A9 (Airstrip #9). I landed my P-51B there, in the land of Lafayette, on July 4, 1944.

From an engineer's point of view, A9 was a challenging project. It required bulldozing part of an apple orchard and building the runway on rather sandy soil, using wire mesh, hammered down with pegs and clamps, to fortify the ground. Not the smoothest landing, but functional enough.

General Omar Bradley located his headquarters at A9, which resulted in quite a string of VIPs touching down at our modest base of operations. England's most famous general, "Monty" Montgomery, would frequently fly in to see Bradley, even though his troops were more to the east, near Caen. Whenever a VIP was scheduled to arrive, we scrambled a flight of Mustangs to supply air cover in case the Germans had intercepted the radio message.

Our most prestigious VIPs were nothing less than, quite arguably, the two most important men of the 20th century, Churchill and Eisenhower. Every few days, Ike and the British Bulldog (as the Russians called Churchill) would fly across the Channel to meet with Bradley. Their silver B-25 would glide in for a routine landing, and then all the GIs gathered around and cheered, as the two grand old men acknowledged them with a smile and a wave before making the short walk to Bradley's headquarters.

My sergeant took these pictures and gave me prints for my records. Churchill's and Eisenhower's expressions convey quite a lot, I think. The war was certainly not over in early August 1944, but a corner had been turned, and you can see their genuine smiles and relaxed postures. They knew that our foothold in Europe would hold.

A CONNECTICUT YANKEE IN KING GEORGE'S COURT

Captain George James came from upstate New York, but that didn't stop us from giving him the nickname of a Wild West desperado. Everybody called him Jesse. He hated cold weather and vowed he would move to a warmer clime if he made it through the war.

When it came to naming his plane, Jesse took a bit more personal approach than the B-17 and other bomber crews, who would often picture a scantily clad girl on the fuselage. We had a few like that, too, in air reconnaissance, but on the whole, we were quite a bit less flamboyant. Hope was the name of Jesse's wife; Jollie, the name of his daughter. And Faith? Exactly what it says—Faith that he would make it home, and be able to see, for the first time, that very same daughter, who was born four months after Jesse left for England.

Jesse was a real Connecticut Yankee. He had a remarkable aptitude for mechanical invention, a talent that he put to good use just after D-Day. In preparation for the landing on Normandy, the Army decided to attach a long copper tube, five to six feet tall and about the diameter of a dime, to the engines of jeeps and other vehicles making an amphibious landing. Basically the tube worked like a snorkel to keep the surf out and let air into the carburetor when the jeep exited the landing craft and hit the beach with the engine running. Once the vehicle was safely ashore, the copper tubing had outlived its purpose, so the GIs would snip them off with a pair of pliers. There were five-foot sections of copper tubing lying around all over the place.

That's when Jesse got the idea to build a contraption that would supply us with hot water—not for bathing, but for shaving. As pilots, we preferred to be clean-shaven because wearing your mask over a five-day growth could be very irritating, and shaving with cold water was irritating as well.

Jesse's invention worked like a charm. You brought your own supply of cold water in your steel helmet and poured it into a reservoir, a 6" x 6" GI can. The water would drain down into the copper tubing, where it was heated by a pressure gas burner. A vacuum brought the hot water to a valve. Turn it and, voila! It was very popular, and Jesse was really proud of it. We had hot water in the middle of a French apple orchard about 200 yards from the Normandy beaches. We thought we were living like kings.

George flew about 70 missions I would say. Then one day he announced, "That's it. I can't fly any more." You can't blame a man for that. The war was coming to an end. He had done more than his part. He had kept the faith. Now he wanted to see his Hope and Jollie. True to his word, Jesse returned home and soon moved to North Carolina and warmer weather. He still lives there today.

Yankee Ingenuity: Jesse James' hot water machine.

"C'EST MOI."

Little did I know when I took this photograph (*left*) of Louise Marie and her daughter, Denise, in Normandy that it would lead to our reunion 50 years later.

Shortly after the end of World War II, many of the cities in France, Belgium and other countries in Western Europe began to reach out to America and its allies, a natural outpouring of genuine emotion and appreciation for their liberators from Hitler's Nazi aggression. As a result of these efforts, Nashville and Caen, a city in France, became Sister Cities.

In October 1993, Dominique Maugeais, a young attorney from Caen, came to Nashville as a member of a delegation from her city for the purpose of encouraging the Sister Cities relationship. Prior to their visit, Lonnie Frey, an active member of the Sister Cities organization, had learned of my collection of war photographs. She arranged for Phyllis Pennington to make enlargements of a number of these photographs to display at a gathering of the visitors from Caen. The photograph of Louise Marie captured Dominique's interest. She requested a copy of the picture, saying she would find the lady in the portrait made fifty years ago. She took the photograph to the weekly newspaper in Le Molay-Littry. When it appeared on the front page, Louise Marie called the editor and said simply, "C'est moi."

Louise Marie and her daughter, Denise, in 1944.

The following week, two photographs appeared in the newspaper, the one taken in 1944, and the follow-up picture taken in 1994 of Louise Marie and her grown daughter, Denise Guerin, now with four sons of her own.

The outcome of this moving story was somewhat remarkable. Jean Mombrun, an enthusiastic historian of World War II, arranged for my wife and me to revisit Le Molay-Littry. He and his wife Madeleine, as well as the Guerins, served as our gracious hosts. Jean also planned an exhibition, which included about 70 of my photographs, to celebrate the 50th anniversary of D-Day. The townspeople and the mayor welcomed us with enthusiastic gratitude. One very special lady, Jeanine Gillingham, the widow of an American soldier, was our valuable and delightful interpreter at the numerous celebration gatherings. Since our visit, a number of Nashvillians have been recipients of her warm hospitality, as well as that of Jean Mombrun.

Louise Marie and her daughter, Denise, fifty years later.
We found them during our trip to Normandy for the
50th anniversary of D-Day.

"A VOTRE SANTE"

I've read with interest the recent reports of commercial pilots who were caught drinking alcohol mere hours before their scheduled flight. They were not the first to exhibit such an egregious lack of judgment. For in 1944, in a small Normandy village, I found myself in a similar situation, though one, I can fortunately say, almost entirely not of my own making.

My trouble began from an unlikely source: the very likable Doc Trimble. Doc was our squadron's physician, a position that caused him great frustration. As air reconnaissance pilots, it seems, we either made it back in one piece or we didn't. Occasionally, there would be a piece of flak to remove, but that was about the extent of it. In short, Doc was bored, but wanting to be of some use to somebody, he would invariably find ways to help people in whatever town or village that happened to be nearby.

Such was the case when Doc met a woman in the village. One day she and her husband brought their young daughter to see Doc. The girl was suffering from a skin infection, possibly eczema, and Doc gave her some GI salve. It worked. In three of four days the rash was gone. Before I knew it, Doc was inviting me to a little celebration party the family was hosting to express their appreciation.

I was invited, I think, because I spoke a little French. We gathered together at one in the afternoon for what I was hoping would be just a short, but friendly, visitation. In any case, if the festivities became prolonged, I had a legitimate excuse to leave early: I was scheduled to fly a mission in an hour.

Minutes after we arrived, the husband produced a tall bottle filled with a clear syrupy liquid. Suddenly, tiny little liquor glasses were passed around. A toast to the health of his little girl would soon be in order.

I explained my situation to Doc, that I was scheduled to fly in less than an hour. Doc was completely unsympathetic. "You cannot deny the hospitality of this French farmer," he said. "It would be an insult to him and his family."

I protested but to no avail. "I'll ground you if you don't drink it," Doc warned. The glasses were filled, and I made a toast, "A votre sante!" "To your health!"

I took one sip, which nearly blew the top of my head off. My palate was full of fire and then a sensation of intense warmth filled my belly. Being from Tennessee, I thought perhaps I was drinking some French version of American moonshine. I later discovered that I had been drinking calvados, an apple brandy.

Because none of our guests spoke English, Doc and I were able to converse freely. "I can't drink any more of this stuff," I said. "It'll knock me out."

"You must drink it all," Doc commanded, with a grimace.

So there I was, trying to carry on a polite conversation in my broken French with a Southern accent, sipping on this homemade concoction and wondering how I would manage to fly a plane over enemy territory with my head in the clouds.

As we returned to the base, I pleaded with Doc to scrub me from the mission. "C'mon Doc," I said. "You've got to ground me." My pleading fell on deaf ears.

Fortunately, the mission was scrubbed for other reasons. Otherwise, there was a pretty good chance I would not have come back in one piece.

Doc Trimble (*right*), our squadron's physician, with a mock demonstration of his job responsibilities.

Piccadilly Circus in London.

A French mother with her two
daughters in Normandy.

140 HOLES

In the heartless arena of war, the difference between living and dying is measured in almost imperceptibly small units. A rifleman aims and fires his weapon, and whether the bullet grazes the flesh or pierces the heart of the human target depends entirely on when enough pressure is applied by the nervous, sweaty trigger finger of an 18-year-old boy. Such are the unforgiving contingencies of combat.

A mere five feet determined my fate. Or to express it in more precisely calibrated terms, 1/50 of a second: the time it took my plane, flying at approximately 180 mph, to travel that same five feet and occupy that exact coordinate in the sky where German anti-aircraft fire destroyed my plane's camera, instead of me.

The standard procedure for an air reconnaissance mission was to use two planes. The #1 pilot was responsible for taking the aerial photographs. The #2 pilot served as a lookout, flying above his companion and keeping an eye out for enemy planes as well as anti-aircraft batteries on the ground.

For this particular mission, I was breaking in a new #1 pilot named Lieutenant Sergeant. All I can say is that he should have stayed a sergeant. We were flying over northern France to check on enemy movements. The Allies had just launched a breakthrough offensive south of Cherbourg, one that would eventually lead us to almost surrounding the German army at the Falaise Pocket.

When you're flying reconnaissance, your first priority, once you arrive in the general vicinity of your mission, is to orient yourself by identifying a specific town or landmark. That was Lieutenant Sergeant's job, but as I was flying at 3,500 feet as the #2, it became painfully obvious that Lieutenant Sergeant was lost. He kept circling a town—once, twice, three times. Becoming increasingly frustrated, I finally called him over the radio and said, "Let me take over."

I had hardly uttered those words when a violent explosion rocked my plane. Like patient hunters waiting for a pair of doves to come within their range, a German anti-aircraft battery had opened fire. The noise was deafening. Black flak was everywhere. I felt shrapnel rip through the fuselage. The engine sputtered to a stop, and the plane started to fall. I opened the cockpit, took off my helmet and prepared to jump. Then, inexplicably, the engine started up again. I quickly put my helmet back on, called in "May Day" to the airstrip and dropped the nose of the plane, forcing the German gunners to readjust their sights.

I had 20 miles to make it to the airstrip. As I grew closer, rather than circling the field and lining up with the runway, I came in at an angle. Wheels down. Flaps down. I thought I was safe. Then, 50 feet above the runway, the engine gave out completely. I coasted in, landing the plane dead stick. Unbeknownst to me, the shrapnel had severed one of the hydraulic brake lines, so when I tried to stop, I ground-looped the plane and made an abrupt turn to the right. Out of control, heading straight for a rock wall, I stopped 10 feet short.

The ground crew and ambulance raced toward me, but I just sat in the plane. A few minutes later my sergeant came up to me. "Major," he said,"I counted 140 holes in your plane. I don't know how you got her back."

The best we could tell, the flak exploded just below and behind me. It destroyed the $10,000 reconnaissance camera located five feet behind my seat and just in front of the tail wheel. I still have a piece of film, shot through with shrapnel, from the camera. At the bottom, my sergeant scratched in the date: July 30, 1944.

Some people would say that was my lucky day. For me, it's the day God smiled on Joe Thompson.

THE FALAISE POCKET

After an initial thrust inland from the Normandy beaches, Allied Forces made little progress in June and July, stymied by the thick French hedgerows and a mighty German army still possessed with a will to fight. Then, on July 25, 1944, Patton launched Operation Cobra, breaking through the German lines between the villages of Marigny and St. Gilles, after heavy saturation bombing, then driving hard south. By July 31, American tanks and half-tracks occupied the port of Avranches.

Ever the relentless attacker, Patton moved south out of Avranches on August 1 through a narrow opening in the lines. The 100,000 men and some 10,000 vehicles of the newly formed Third Army then fanned out in three columns to the south and southeast. Hitler, against the advice of his best generals, who wanted to retreat and regroup, demanded that Avranches be retaken and the Americans driven into the sea. On August 7, the Germans launched a furious counter-attack at Mortain. Four Panzer divisions were moved up to make the attack, concealed by a thick mist.

The missions posted on August 8 called for my squadron, code name Peafowl Yellow, to report in detail the enemy action in Section 6, the lower part of Normandy, including Avranches and Mortain. At this point, we knew nothing of the German counterattack. We took a route west of St. Lo, now totally destroyed, and quickly reached Villedieu les Poelies, a small town on the rail line between Granville and Vire. Fifteen miles to the south was Mortain. When we encountered some patches of woods, we went down for a closer look and saw armored columns clogging the road advancing for the counterattack. Just 100 feet in the air, we roared above the German soldiers. I could see them scrambling to take a shot at us, but to no avail. We were long gone.

I pulled up sharply, zigzagging like crazy to avoid the flak. I spotted a squadron of P-47 fighter-bombers, perhaps a mile away and waggled my wings to attract their attention since we were not on the same radio frequency. They soon got the message to follow me, and we led the P-47s to the attacking column. Down they dove, machine guns blazing, dropping the 50-pound bombs they carried under each wing.

The mist cleared later that day, and our fighter-bombers were able to destroy 150 German tanks in just a few hours.

Their efforts, as well as the fearless defense of the 30th Infantry Division at Mortain, foiled the counterattack and set the stage for the Falaise Pocket. By advancing so far westward, the failed German counterattack had left their forces highly exposed, and the Allies moved quickly to encircle them.

From the south Patton continued to move at such a furious speed that even Allied officers were prone not to believe reports of his position.

Sometime during the middle of August, on the last air reconnaissance flight of the day, a young first lieutenant (whose name I unfortunately can't remember) and his #2 flew out to identify Patton's most current position. After landing back at A9, he hurried to Bradley's headquarters, where a group of high-ranking officers were gathered around a huge map on a large table.

"General Patton's lead tanks are here," he said, pointing to a spot not far from Chartres. "Tomorrow, they will be past Chartres and probably beyond Paris."

Confusion and disbelief enveloped the entire room. A colonel leaned forward to point to Patton's presumed position. "There's no way Patton has advanced that far," he said. "Those must be German tanks you saw."

The young lieutenant stood his ground. "Colonel, I know a German tank when I see one. These <u>are</u> Patton's tanks. The lead tank had a fluorescent marking. This is where he is, and this is where he will be in 24 hours."

The young lieutenant was right, of course, and Bradley's staff exulted.

On August 16, seeing that all was lost, Hitler ordered a withdrawal. By this time, the Germans' only path of retreat was a small opening, aptly named the Corridor of Death, which was attacked repeatedly by our fighter-bombers. However, because of communication misunderstandings, we didn't manage to completely close the Falaise Pocket until August 21. Although we did capture 150,000 men, two German divisions escaped, and those same 100,000 troops would reappear, to our great consternation, in the Battle of the Bulge

But for now, the Battle of Normandy had been won. Now it was on to Paris.

THE LIBERATION OF PARIS

On September 2, 1944, we moved our operations to Buc Airdrome, on the edge of Paris, near the palace of Versailles. In an attempt to camouflage the airfield, the Germans had planted rows of potatoes between the runways. As soon as we arrived, the locals, now feeling secure, ventured out, wheelbarrows in tow, to dig them up. We dug up some ourselves, slicing them up to make what the French call "Les Frites."

For several days, there were no missions to fly. The German lines were so close that air reconnaissance was not required. We had two days off; it was time to see Paris. For the most part, the Germans left Paris as they found it, and the heart of the city had been spared from Allied bombing. There was only an occasional reminder of the Nazi's extended stay, a burned out Tiger tank, for example, abandoned in the Place de la Concorde. Hitler had ordered the city destroyed, leading to his famous question "Is Paris burning?" Fortunately, Choltitz, the German garrison commander, refused to obey the order.

Upon our arrival, we came upon a parade celebrating the city's liberation. Parisians lined the sidewalk as the Allied soldiers walked and drove by in a miscellaneous collection of vehicles. Young French women kept pulling the GIs out of the parade to express their gratitude with a passionate kiss, and the GIs gladly obliged. In a show of unity, tanks from each of the Allied nations were lined up under the Arc de Triomphe in a mock re-enactment of the Germans' triumphant entry four years earlier. A patriotic Frenchman, carried away by the exuberance of the moment, walked up the stairs inside the monument and then managed to hang his national banner, replacing the Nazi flag that had been disgracefully displayed for so long on this symbol of French national pride.

Joy reigned, and yet, just a few blocks away from where this picture was taken, war still raged. A group of German soldiers, staying in a hotel of somewhat ill-repute, had not gotten the word to withdraw, and the French Underground was busy cleaning up the area, which we were told to stay clear of, their efforts peppering the air with the sound of an occasional rifle shot.

In the midst of all this exuberance, a young, rather wealthy Frenchman invited a group of officers for a celebration party at his house, just 1/2 mile from the Eiffel Tower. With the city still lacking electricity, candles illuminated the house. Wine flowed, soldiers danced, couples embraced, but civility, not debauchery, ruled the day: none of the women were allowed to leave the dance floor area.

Eventually duty called. Sometime after midnight, my squad members and I returned to our jeep. To prevent it from being stolen, a common occurrence, we had removed the rotor from the distributor so the plugs wouldn't fire. I replaced the rotor and tried to start the engine. Nothing. We looked under the hood. Someone had torn out the thick piece of wire that connects the coil to the distributor, probably to spite us for having disabled the engine and thwarting their attempt to steal it. I knocked on my host's door, asking for a certain diameter piece of wire, but my broken, southern French and the fact that I did not know the French word for "wire" hindered our communication. Eventually, he understood what I was trying to say and found a piece of wire, 2 1/2 feet long. It was smaller in diameter than the original, but I thought it might work.

It did, sort of. With the City of Lights under a complete blackout, we negotiated strange and unfamiliar streets, the rough cobblestone pavement causing the makeshift coil to pop off constantly, killing the engine. We would tumble out of the jeep to search the streets with our pocket flashlights for that little piece of wire until someone yelled, "I found it." Four times we went through this absurd exercise, laughing all the way, feeling for a moment, like college kids on an adventure, instead of soldiers in a war.

Various tanks from each of the Allied nations gathered under the Arc de Triomphe during the celebration of the liberation of Paris. Note the French flag at the top.

BUZZING THE EIFFEL TOWER

Shortly after arriving at the Buc Airdrome, at the green age of 25, with little more than two years experience as a commissioned officer, I was made CO of the squadron, in charge of 40 pilots and some 250 support personnel. How did I achieve this prestigious command at such a young age? Was I somehow now being recognized for my leadership ability or being rewarded for the numerous missions I had flown?

Hardly. This promotion was really all about the cruel mathematics of war. With the number of pilots that had been killed or captured, transferred to shore up a more decimated squadron or to help form a new one, sent home on Section 8 (mentally unable to continue) or moved up to a higher command, I was about the only one left. I had the assistance of an older executive officer, who helped me run the ground operations, Otherwise, it was up to me and my good friend from North Dakota, Paul Ebeltoft, to run the show.

The escapades of a handsome young pilot presented the first opportunity to exercise my new authority. In much the same way that a young 15-year-old boy suddenly is seized with the idea of taking his father's car out for a ride, this wild-eyed pilot decided he wanted to buzz the Eiffel Tower, not realizing, unfortunately, that guy wires are used to stabilize the 900-foot structure. One of his wings hit a guy wire, but somehow he managed to stay in the air and land at our small airbase, crammed with airplanes that lined the runways. A hydraulic brake line had been severed by the collision, so when he tried to stop, he promptly ground looped, but ended up neatly and miraculously parked between two planes.

As this was my first attempt at disciplining someone as the CO, I tried to be as intimidating as possible, but I was not comfortable with the role of playing the heavy.

GOSSELIES - HOME AWAY FROM HOME

The small Belgian town of Gosselies was our home for much of
the winter of 1944-45. Note the German camouflage netting still
in place at top.

A HERO'S WELCOME

By September 1944, with the Germans retreating through France and Belgium, it became necessary to move our operations to a new base, closer to the front lines, in order to provide more efficient air reconnaissance. Such decisions were made on a rather informal basis. Higher-ups notified our group CO, who then informed the squadron leaders that we needed to check out a potential airbase in Belgium. Within a matter of an hour, four of us were flying to a destination known only to the group CO, and within 20 minutes we were circling a camouflaged air field in the bend of a river next to the little town of Gosselies, Belgium.

When we flew over the airstrip, which was nothing more than a small, grassy field, we were surprised to see civilians there, little figures meandering about on the field like ants in the grass. Needing to land and take a look around, we buzzed the airfield to inform them of our intentions, but the Belgians just waved and cheered. We landed anyway, with the civilians scattering to safety like a covey of quail, and taxied over to a concrete parking area built by the Germans.

And then, for the first and only time in my life, I was welcomed as a hero. Almost before the prop stopped turning, a crowd had gathered around my plane—happy, shouting, smiling Belgians, bringing with them bottles of beer, grapes and whatever else they could offer as tribute, which they promptly plopped in my lap as soon as I opened the plane's canopy. We were overwhelmed by the unexpected expression of thanks and tried to communicate, as best we could, that we were pleased that they were pleased. We looked around briefly and, finding the airstrip acceptable to our needs, said good-bye to our new admirers and roared off into the sky.

Two days later, the entire squadron landed at our new base, and I was soon to learn the dark source of the deep and sincere gratitude with which this town embraced us.

A COMMON SHALLOW GRAVE

The Nazis had occupied Gosselies for some 3 1/2 years, and during that time, many of the townspeople had simply disappeared. Soon after our arrival, the mayor of the town and several other local leaders made a formal request to dig up a plot of earth that they feared, with near certainty, contained the bodies of their missing neighbors.

They were right, of course. The shallow common grave, about 60 yards long, was located in the middle of the airstrip among our planes and equipment. For several days, the people of this small and friendly town got on with the grisly task of exhuming the bodies and identifying their neighbors and loves ones. Family members brought flags and flowers to the site. Some 190 people were murdered, including many married couples, whose children were now orphans.

A few months later, when Christmas rolled around, we held a holiday party for these orphaned children, complete with food, presents and a GI dressed up as Santa Claus. About a month later, just before our squadron left, the people of Gosselies presented us with a thank-you card, which all the children of the village had signed.

We were moved to tears.

Some 40 years later, our adjutant, Captain Pennington, who had received the present, sent me the thank-you card, which he had found among his personal papers. I in turn sent it to the squadron museum in St. Paul, Minnesota, where you can still see it today.

One of the children of Gosselies.

58

LIFE AT GOSSELIES

Shortly after our arrival in Gosselies, two attractive young ladies, Ann Marie Quinet and her sister, Andre Quinet, greeted us and offered their services as interpreters, since both of them spoke fluent English.

During their occupation, the Germans had banned any public gathering. A party, therefore, was in order, complete with a little GI band, dancing, food and of course, American boy meets Belgian girl. Some of our GIs had little French phrase books, which they would consult quite frequently as they slow danced and tried to maintain eye contact.

All was not fun and games, however. Guilt and retribution made an appearance, too. I noticed a small group of women who kept to themselves, standing around the tables laden with food, which they shortly began stuffing into their pockets. An older Belgian woman approached the group, began arguing with one of the girls and then, to our surprise, yanked off a wig to reveal a shaven head. These women had been German collaborators, and their heads had been shaved to serve as a shameful badge of their betrayal.

Another party provided a more humorous occasion. Fraternization with the locals was a more common occurrence that I care to admit. Our #2 administrative officer had such an arrangement with a local female, who was going to sing for us at the party.

Before she could, however, a very inebriated GI made his way to the front of the room and, grasping the microphone to keep his balance, announced to the crowd, "Ladies and gentleman, it is our distinct honor to have a great singer perform for us this evening. Would you please welcome Madame Couchez Avec." Literally translated: Mrs. Sleep With. Somehow our drunken GI escaped any punishment.

During their unwelcome stay, the Germans had billeted their troops in several buildings, which we now occupied. Unlike the Germans, however, we paid rent. I intended to stay in these lodgings, until a Mr. Eyers, who lived in the house that adjoined our makeshift barracks, insisted that I use the master bedroom in his residence. This would be no hardship at all, he explained, for the local German Commandant had lived there for the past 3 1/2 years, a most unhappy experience. The arrogant interloper had made himself completely at home. He had a key to the house, but many nights he came home so drunk that he was unable to work the latch and would bang on the door until Mr. Eyers, roused from his sleep, opened it. Then, adding insult to injury, he would command Mr. Eyers to take off his muddy boots.

Mr. Eyers, who spoke some English, having served in the British Merchant Marine during World War I, was very insistent about my moving in. "Monseiur Le Major," as he called me, "It is an honor."

And so I did.

Mr. Eyers and his wife kindly allowed me to stay in their Gosselies home.

THE KIND JEWISH MASTER SERGEANT

Across from our headquarters, in this little village we now called home, was a school run by Catholic nuns. Many of the town's orphaned children attended this school. We had a Jewish master sergeant in our unit who had a real concern for these children. For example, he was always asking permission to give the nuns the last 10 or 12 pounds of a 40-pound can of lard, an almost unobtainable luxury, given the scarcity of supplies. About a week later, three nuns, dressed in their formal giant white headdresses, came to see me, accompanied by the Sergeant.

"The nuns have a presentation to make to you," said the sergeant, and with that brief introduction, the nuns presented me with a St. Christopher medal, which they placed around my neck with great ceremony. I figured I needed all the help I could get, and any kind of protection from any segment of the Christian faith was welcome.

We were feeding 300 men three times a day at Gosselies. But under military rules, to prevent the spread of food poisoning, all leftovers had to be thrown out. This immense waste of food appalled our kind Jewish sergeant. He notified the small Belgian Red Cross office in the village that we could provide food to the citizens if they would take care of the transportation and distribution. Not expecting much, the Red Cross workers showed up carrying a few buckets, but their eyes widened in amazement when they saw the volume of food available. And so, thanks to our kind sergeant, the 109th squadron of the Army Air Force fed some 300 Belgians three times a day for two months.

This poker scene needed some visual interest. So I called over one of the players and told him to grab the pot on my cue. Nobody else knew what was going on, and the captain grabbing my actor's sleeve isn't about to let him get away with it.

A TRIP TO BRUSSELS

One of our group COs, in addition to being an able commander, was, to put it discreetly, a ladies man. He called me one evening to see if I was up for an excursion into Brussels. British troops had just recently entered the Belgian capital city on September 4. Knowing that he would probably not return until the next morning, I was reluctant to go until I found a ride back.

We rode in a command car, some five or six of us. Even with the recent Nazi evacuation and the ravages of war, Brussels bustled with an amazing assortment of bars, taverns, nightclubs and eateries. With great alacrity and efficiency, people were getting on with their lives. They were ready to celebrate.

We ended up in a nightclub (and that is a generous description) with a plentiful supply of beer, wine and young ladies eager to dance. I soon found myself paired with a gaudily painted up Belgian girl who spoke no English, but she danced reasonably well, and communication was not the primary objective that night. Our stepping out on the dance floor aroused the smirks and laughter of my companions, who noticed my reluctance.

When the music stopped, my new girlfriend flitted back to my table with complete self-assurance, and it became obvious that she and her companions had their own agenda: to encourage us to drink up and part with our money.

The music was provided by an ancient record player, attended by a female who seemed to be the proprietor or at least in charge of the place. Each time she changed the record, there was a moment of quiet and then a few seconds of the needle scratching its way through the grooves to the music.

We were waiting for the music to begin when something extraordinary happened. Suddenly, blaring out into every inch of air in this cramped and smoky room, we heard the unmistakable sound of a German march. It startled everyone. One could almost see columns of German soldiers parading down the streets of Brussels. The record-changing woman looked in horror at the female co-worker apparently in charge of the record selection. Then she rushed over to the record player and smashed the offending piece of vinyl on her knee as she vehemently screamed something in French. Just a few weeks earlier, no doubt, this establishment had been serving up drinks to German officers, who had danced with these same girls and sat at these same tables.

We got up, picked up our hats and walked out of that place.

BUYING CHEAP CHAMPAGNE

Maintaining high morale is an important priority for a squadron CO. At least that's the way Ebeltoft and I figured it. And what could lift the spirits of our GIs faster and higher than a party, discreet of course, with music, girls and our own bar serving up champagne?

Convinced by our rationalizations, Ebeltoft took off in a 6X6 truck headed to Rhiens, home of a famous champagne winery. He left with 20,000 French francs in his pockets, about $100 collected from our squadron. He came back with the truck fully loaded with champagne bottles in their little straw cases, and very proud of his achievement. The champagne, Gordon Rouge '37, a very fine brand and date, came at a bargain price because of a red label that read "Reserved for the Wehrmacht." Obviously, the French champagne makers were eager to get rid of this embarrassing vintage and at a very good price.

When our champagne supply was running low, Ebeltoft collected another $100 and took off for another champagne run. But this time, he returned with the truck only 2/3 full. When asked "Why the lighter load?" Ebeltoft replied, "I'll show you." He walked around to the back of the truck, pulled out a bottle and showed the new label that said "Reserved for the Allied Armies. "They jacked the price up 30 percent on us just because they changed the label," muttered Ebeltoft in exasperation.

Nowadays I believe they call that good marketing.

THE BATTLE OF THE BULGE

During the first few months of our stay in Gosselies, there were fewer major combat operations in the European Theater. The Germans had retreated to the relative safety of the Siegfried Line, a matrix of reinforced bunkers, pill boxes, concrete entrenchments and tunnels, built opposite the French Maginot Line during the 1930s. Our main reconnaissance missions involved photographing this impressive line of fortifications, which, from the air, looked like a long row of jagged dragon's teeth. The Allied Forces, in turn, were busy shoring up their supply lines that now extended some 40 miles inland from the beaches of Normandy. It was this relative calm, perhaps, that allowed us to form such a strong of bond of friendship and camaraderie with the people of Gosselies.

All that changed however, when the Germans initiated a final desperate counteroffensive to stop the Allied advance and sue for peace: the Battle of the Bulge. Launched on December 16, 1944, the Battle of the Bulge is often characterized as a "surprise attack." By my count, it wasn't. Two weeks prior to battle, our reconnaissance missions documented increased troop movement and vehicle traffic that <u>should</u> have forewarned our superiors.

The Germans launched their attack as that of the Ardennes Forest, the site of a bloody battle in World War I. With its heavily forested terrain, the area seemed an unlikely site for an offensive. As a result, the American line was stretched thin, less than half the concentration of forces compared to other positions on the front line. Almost 1,000,000 men fought in this battle, the costliest of the war in terms of American casualties.

The lead tanks were American, seized earlier and repaired, and the crews wore American uniforms, strictly against Geneva Convention. A sizable number of U.S. troops were caught off guard—and the Nazis, not wanting to be burdened with the handling of prisoners, brutally killed a sizeable number (the Malmady Massacre).

Minutes before I came upon this scene, a German sniper in the church tower had shot an MP on the street. I witnessed the sniper being killed, falling from the tower and hitting the ground. Taking the place of his fallen comrade, another MP stands guard next to the jeep.

Just before the Battle of the Bulge, I received a five-day pass. Our flight surgeon had put in the request, to my surprise. He said I needed it.

And so, on December 19, as I was catching my second wind in London, Allied commanders were meeting in a bunker in Verdun to determine the best response to the German counterattack. Eisenhower asked Patton, whose Third Army then occupied south central France, how long it would take for him to launch a counterattack. Patton's reply— 48 hours—stunned the generals present. The idea was inconceivable. In fact, Patton, anticipating Eisenhower's decision, had already ordered his troops to move.

Patton's forces were rushing to the aid of the 101st Airborne and segments of the 10th Armored Division, who were being encircled by German forces in and around the town of Bastogne. On December 21, the Germans completely surrounded the American forces and demanded their surrender, to which the commanding officer, General Anthony McAuliffe issued a written one-word reply, "Nuts."

The situation was becoming desperate for the men of Bastogne. Patton's forces were just beginning to engage the enemy, who were continuing to advance and bring up reinforcements. In particular, a large German tank force was progressing steadily to the little town of Stavelot, only 22 miles from a vital U.S. supply station and ammunition depot at Liege. Losing Liege would force the entire First Army to retreat.

At this critical juncture in the war, two of our pilots, Cassidy and Jaffee, played a pivotal role in the Battle of the Bulge. The head of the IX Tactical Air Command, Major General Elwood Ricardo Quesada, asked for volunteers to fly in the foggy soup and try to locate the German column advancing toward Stavelot. Cassidy and Jaffe stepped forward.

With the clouds almost at treetop level, so low that "Even the birds are walking," as someone quipped, Cassidy and Jaffe were able to fly a mission, following the valley contours of this landscape they knew so well. They spotted an advancing Panzer tank division, then led our P-47 fighters to rain down upon them with their 50-lb bombs, two per plane. When darkness halted the attack, the Allied fighters counted 126 enemy tanks, armored vehicles and trucks destroyed, with 34 more damaged. No German tank made it much beyond Stavelot. The advance had been stopped.

You may never read about Cassidy and Jaffee in any accounts of the Battle of the Bulge, but in my mind, they were a deciding factor in the ultimate Allied victory.

At about this point, just as I returned to England, I participated in a dramatic midnight meeting. Standing on the front esplanade of a magnificent ancient chateau, our group CO explained the situation: German forces were advancing toward the Meuse River near the city of Namur. If they succeeded in crossing the river, only about 15 miles away, and reaching the airfield, each man would be responsible for destroying his plane. (The overcast conditions prohibited us from flying away.) For the next three hours, we wondered if we might be fighting Panzer tanks with our meager carbine rifles.

Fortunately, the Germans did not cross, their efforts stymied by Patton's courageous march and the men of Bastogne. By December 23, the weather conditions improved, and the P-47s continued their devastating bombardment of the German troops and tanks. On Christmas Eve, the German advance stalled, and the first half of the Battle of the Bulge was history.

THE FINAL PUSH

Vapor trails of the B-17s, and the smaller trails of their
fighter escorts, waiting until all the planes in the vast
armada had taken off and joined the formation to fly to
the Rhine Valley.

THE CARROT BEFORE THE HORSE

For a soldier, hope is the food of the soul. Without it, you die spiritually. Without a tangible belief that this ongoing hell surrounding you each day will someday cease, you gradually begin to feel like a condemned man facing an uncertain but inevitable date of demise.

The army understood this, and so they created the "tour of duty." For members of a long-range bomber crew, it was 25 missions. For medium-range bomber crews, it was 50 missions. There it was, dangling before your mind, just out of your reach, but drawing closer every day. Your tour of duty was your countdown to survival, your ticket back home. It made hope specific and quantifiable, something you could touch: "only nine—seven—two missions to go." Reach that magic number and you'd find yourself back on the front porch at home, sipping lemonade, courting girls and checking the newspapers for baseball scores. The bliss of normalcy, now fully appreciated, would be yours to partake of—completely.

For aerial reconnaissance pilots, however, hope was in short supply. For reasons still unknown to me, there was no prescribed tour of duty for a squadron of our type. Apparently, our mission was to dart and soar above the Nazi-occupied skies, forever taking photographs until the war ended.

Either someone thought our casualty rate did not warrant a tour of duty, or they simply forgot to establish one, since our numbers, compared to the bomber squadrons, were so small.

At first, this oversight was of no concern. But now that there were men in the squadron who had flown 40, 50, even 60 combat missions, the CO's pleaded with our commanders for a tour of duty to be instituted. After some delay, we received our magical number: 75 missions, no doubt concocted by some bureaucrat who liked the symmetry it created: 25, 50, 75.

Inexorably, as the days passed and missions were flown, members of my squadron moved closer and closer to grabbing the brass ring. A few pilots even reached the 75-mission milestone, and they were sent home with great acclamation. But the higher-ups were just as aware as we were of what the score was and how many men were about to qualify. Not wanting to suffer a pilot shortage, they shortly thereafter increased the requirement for our tour of duty to 80 missions, then later to 85 missions and finally to 90. But by then, the war was over. And that was, after all, the only carrot the horses really wanted.

KRAUTBALLS

Starting at Gosselies and continuing to the end of the war, men in my squadron would return from their missions and report seeing what they described as "silver footballs in the sky." Some called them Foo Fighters, a term picked up from the pre-war Smokey Stover comic strip. Others called them Krautballs. We didn't know what they were, but we knew they were real: there were too many reports to discount them as hallucinations or one-time aberrations. We suspected that they were some kind of secret German weapon, perhaps sent up to help the AA batteries gauge the altitude of our planes. Some in our group suspected the lights might be attached to wires, like barrage balloons, but the lights were too mobile and too high for this to be the case. We heard reports from other squadrons reporting the same phenomenon, including night fighter groups and the 15th Air Force in Italy. We even called up the Third Army to see if they were responsible. Later on, as the Eastern and Western fronts grew nearer, we wondered if the Russians were up to something.

I first saw them flying a mission on a beautiful clear day over the Rhine Valley. There they were at about 6,000 to 7,000 feet altitude, five or six silvery saucers. They moved up and down like a boxer bobbing and weaving, all in unison as if they were tied together by a string.

I wanted to investigate, but I couldn't. The mission came first. No one had ever reported being fired upon by these objects, and since nearly everything else in the Rhine Valley had taken the liberty of trying to shoot us down, the silvery balls were of less importance to me than the dangers that lurked in the valley below. But the experience triggered a lifelong interest in UFOs, and I still believe that what I saw that day was not of this world.

THE PIGEON SERGEANT

War is not always fought by the young. One member of our squadron was an old master sergeant from St. Paul, Minnesota. He had been in the National Guard for 20 years or more before the war caught up with him. He was in charge of our armaments, the .50 caliber machine guns carried by every plane, and absolutely reliable at his job. Being much older than the rest of us, he tended to stay to himself, and there was a sense of immense loneliness about him. It seemed as if the only friend he had was a pigeon whom he would feed every day. The pigeon would rest on his arm or shoulder and keep him company, and the two stayed together all the way through Europe.

THE END OF THE LINE

After almost two years of flying combat missions, I had put my P-51 Mustang through a fair share of air acrobatics and maneuvers: 400-mph dives, tight turns and violent zigzags to avoid flak. But sometime during the Battle of the Bulge, on an otherwise routine mission, I encountered, quite unexpectedly, what would eventually be the end of line for me. I got air sick.

I was flying again with Hogan Jones as my #2. Hogan had completed a 75-mission tour of duty before they arbitrarily raised the standard and had returned to the States. That apparently bored him, because he signed up for another tour of duty. At least, that's the only explanation I could think of as to why he re-enlisted.

We were flying over the Rhine Valley, above the jagged teeth of the Siegfried Line, when halfway through the mission, I became severely nauseated. I reluctantly broke off the mission, and Hogan Jones dutifully followed, no doubt wondering what I was up to, but this time managing to keep radio silence. As soon as I crossed the Siegfried Line, however, the nausea seemed to subside, so I turned the plane back again to photograph a bridge on the Rhine River. But soon nausea swept over me again, this time even more severe, and I terminated the mission.

Safely on the ground, I began discussing the mission, as was the usual procedure, with our intelligence officer, Bill Stallworth. During this conversation, I mentioned that I had become air sick twice and speculated that it must have been something I had eaten the night before. I heard a cough in the doorway and looked up to see Doc Trimble standing there.

"All right, Thompson," he said sharply. "That's all for you."

"What are you talking about," I asked.

"What you just described is a textbook case of combat fatigue," he said.

I protested. "C'mon Doc," I said. "It was just indigestion. I'll be all right."

"Thompson," responded Doc, "you're grounded. I don't care if you are the C.O. You're not flying for at least another week and then we'll review it."

Doc, as it turned out, was right. I had already sent three or four pilots home with combat fatigue, and now I had reached my physical limitations. I flew only a few missions after Doc temporarily grounded me, but one of those missions involved nothing less than an encounter with the supernatural.

RIGHT AND UP

Learning the art of flying in combat is, to a large extent, a matter of acquiring the right habits. Whenever possible, procedures are standardized; routines are established. Everything is prescribed so that as little as possible is left to happenstance—all with the specific purpose of avoiding unnecessary mistakes. When an act becomes habitual, it becomes repeatable and predictable. For example, throughout the entire European Theater, all turns were made to the left. When you circled the airport, you turned to the left. When a four-plane fighter position needed to break, they turned to the left. But on February 10, 1945, on one of my last missions, I was told to turn to the right, and that inspired instruction no doubt saved my life.

This particular mission involved photographing for the Merton Oblique. This technique used a specially developed grid that was placed over a series of photographs of the target and allowed the artillery to zero in their guns and hit the prescribed target on the first round. No more firing rounds for position and then firing for effect. The precision of the artillery fired using the Merton Oblique was such that the Germans thought we had developed a secret weapon that guided the rounds using radar.

Although the Merton Oblique was a boon for the artillery, air reconnaissance pilots regarded it with some disfavor. Photographing for the Merton Oblique required a special technique. We had to fly straight and level for up to three minutes at 200 feet. For this particular mission, that path followed a road that paralleled the German front lines. For any German gunner, a plane flying straight and level for three minutes was like shooting fish in a barrel.

But that was the mission. So there I was, coming down from 12,000 feet, making a zigzag pattern until I leveled the plane, found the right heading, turned on the camera and steadied myself for the longest 180 seconds of my life. Behind me, flak bursts began tracking me, increasingly gaining ground. Over the radio, my #2 methodically called out their approach, "50 yards…40 yards…30 yards." The end of the run was near now. Just a few more seconds to complete the mission, then make the standard move—left and up—and get out of there!

Then something amazing happened. Just as I was about to break off my run, something, or somebody, said, "Thompson, break right and up." It was not a voice that came over the ear phones. It was not thunderous and awe-inspiring divine proclamation. It was a still, quiet voice that said these simple words directly, even matter-of-factly. What is even more intriguing is that the voice addressed me in the third person as "Thompson," not a convention of speech that I would have employed if the thought had occurred spontaneously to myself.

So I broke right and up, and then my #2 yelled over the radio," Flak, flak!" I looked to my left, where I should have turned, and the sky was black with AA. The shrewd German gunners had anticipated my move. They assumed I was going left and up, a move that I had made hundreds, even thousands of times, a move that was as predictable and habitual as my picking up a pencil with my right hand or driving on the right side of the road in America.

But the voice had said, "Right and up." And so I did. I was about to turn the wrong way when God intervened and set me right.

This series of photographs clearly demonstrates the physical strain caused by the war.

(L) A young second lieutenant, I had just graduated from Randolph Field, Texas.

(Center) Waking up from my nap on my 25th birthday, June 8, 1944.

(R) By the time we got to Belgium, the war had worked me down to 15 cents.

BURG VOGELSANG (1938)
Mental capacity was secondary.

European

REWRITING HISTORY AT VOGELSANG

After Gosselies, we moved to airbase R11, located next to Ordensburg Vogelsang, the former headquarters of the German SS officer corps. It was here that I took one of my favorite photographs (*page 67*), the vapor trails of the B-17s, and the smaller trails of their fighter escorts, accumulating in the spring sky, created by the first planes of a vast armada, lumbering through the air and circling the field over and over, waiting until all the planes had taken off and joined the formation to fly to the Rhine Valley.

It was also at Vogelsang that I saw for the first time a V-2 rocket. Launched some 100 miles away across the Rhine River, it looked like a giant telephone pole, wandering erratically at first, then straightening up and leaving a jet trail as it ascended 50 miles into the atmosphere, traveling at supersonic speed and striking Hyde Park in London or some other English target, without warning, a mere five minutes after launch.

We were at Vogelsang only about a week, maybe 10 days. I had the opportunity to explore the ruins of the former SS headquarters, intrigued by the idea of investigating this former hang-out for the German elite. I found myself in a bombed-out library, the roof completely blown off by our artillery, the bookshelves in shambles and books scattered everywhere. When I examined them, I found, to my surprise, they were all newly printed, shiny and crisp with their pages unscarred by any human use. Thanks to three years of scientific German at Vanderbilt, I was able to comprehend the basic meaning of each book, and as I leafed through the pages, I slowly discerned that these volumes were a rewriting of human knowledge from the Nazi perspective, every subject reworked to support the existence of an Aryan super race.

I dropped the writings to the floor and left. Years later, I realized these books had what is nicely called "historical significance." But at the time, it seemed only right to return them to the rubble.

Ordensburg Vogelsang, the former headquarters of the German SS officer corps.

WHITE FLAGS AT LIMBERG

Our time at Vogelsang was brief. With the foiling of the Germans' planned demolition of the Remagen Bridge, our Allied forces soon crossed the Rhine River, and our squadron moved to an airdrome near the little town of Limberg, 30 miles east of the Rhine. From here, I flew my last flight in a P-51, an uneventful solo mission that took me over Bonn and Koblenz, all territory controlled by the Allies. It was a strange feeling to fly without the fear of black flak suddenly pummeling the air or expecting a squadron of FW-190s to suddenly appear. I tried to relax, but this new knowledge that I was now flying in friendly skies could not completely overcome my habit of constant vigilance, well honed by 90 previous missions.

The Limburg airdrome was located in a valley, and one day I took a jeep and drove to the top of the hill that overlooked our temporary home. It was early April, and for the first time I noticed German farmers, elderly men, too old for military service, plowing their fields and planting their crops. Affixed to the harness of each horse that pulled the plow was a small white flag that seemed to say, with perfect clarity, "Leave me alone, I'm harmless." Those small white flags, dotting the landscape, filled me with encouragement, for they were the first signs that life was returning to normal.

Gasoline was all you needed to turn a German motorcycle into a popular amusement.

MOTORCYCLES, GLIDERS AND BUZZING
THE BERCHTESGARTEN

War movies are made to entertain, and so they never convey the dreary monotony that comes with being a soldier. There was always plenty of time to kill, and we invented plenty of ways to kill it.

Often, for example, the GIs would find German motorcycles, in good working order, left behind at the different airdromes. They would fill them up with gas and take turns riding them through the hangers (*page 78*).

The most innovative example of GI's trying to have some fun occurred at Limburg. During the later stages of the war, the Germans used gliders to train their young pilots in order to save gasoline. Several of these beautifully built gliders were strewn about the hillside at Limburg, and one glider, near the top of the hill, attracted the attention of two of our most mischievous GIs. A sergeant enlisted the help of a corporal, and together they concocted a seriously flawed scheme for taking a ride in the glider. They drove a jeep up to the glider and attached the two with a long rope. With the sergeant in the glider, the corporal gunned the jeep's motor and took off down the hill.

The glider was so light that it launched immediately into the air, this beautiful red German glider, with a swastika painted on the tail, flying silently and peacefully over the airdrome, and the corporal looking back over his shoulder as he flew down the hill, desperately trying to stay ahead of his fast-moving tow. Unfortunately, the two had forgotten to think about a release system, and at the bottom of the hill, the corporal, running out of real estate, had to slam on the brakes. The glider lost its momentum, dove steeply and clunked into the back of the jeep. Fortunately, no one was hurt by this little entertaining sideshow of the war.

A more dangerous form of "killing time" was undertaken by a P-38 pilot in our squadron. In the last few weeks of the war, he decided he wanted to photograph the Eagle's Nest at Berchtesgarten, Hitler's mountain hideaway in the German Alps. After completing his assigned mission, he flew off course over the German Alps to take this remarkable picture (*left*). Caught completely off guard, the German AA batteries did not fire a shot before the P-38 snapped the shutter of its front-mounted camera and zipped away.

The Eagle's Nest at Berchtesgarten, Hitler's mountain hideaway in the German Alps.

SAVING BRITS AND WATCHING
THE RUSSIANS

From Limberg, it was on to the city of Kassel and our last airdrome of the war, Echwege. For the last 2 1/2 weeks of the war, our only missions involved watching the Russians and making sure they didn't cross the Elbe River and start World War III.

When we first arrived at Echwege, our first job was to sweep the area and make sure it was safe. I remember following a sergeant after he had heard a noise from a building's third floor. We came to a closed door and ordered the unknown occupants to come out, No response. So we kicked open the door, saw nothing, then cautiously approached another room. There, sitting at a table, was a British officer in uniform. Another British officer lay in a bed. They were extremely weak, having been without food or water for at least a day. They were paratroopers, captured at Arnheim. I offered one a bar of chocolate, but he wisely refused. Such rich food was not what was needed in his weakened condition. Soon, our doctor took over and gave them some barley soup to sip.

The war was nearly over now, and from the air you could see long lines of German troops, marching toward the Allied lines to surrender. The Germans always headed west, toward the Allies. They did not want to surrender to the Russians, whose land had been ravaged by Hitler's 1942 offensive. More than any other people, the Russians suffered most from the war, with over 6,000,000 battle deaths. They were ripe for revenge.

Once, a German JU-88, a twin-engine bomber and, at the time, one of the finest aircrafts in the world, buzzed our airdrome at such a low altitude that our AA batteries had no opportunity to fire.

It quickly landed on the grass next to the runway with its wheels up, mangling the propeller, but otherwise suffering no other damage. The side door popped open, and out stepped two German officers, with their wives and children, all with broad smiles and their hands up to surrender.

Though now nearly decimated, the Luftwaffe still put up a fight, sending up pilots as young as 15 years old, with so little flying instruction that they were doing well just to keep the plane straight and level. Two pilots encountered an ME-109 obviously being flown by one of these boy pilots, for when they engaged the plane, it did not attempt any evasive maneuvers. Instead of destroying the plane, however, the two pilots positioned themselves on either wing of the plane and motioned to the pilot to land. As the three-plane formation made its approach, the two pilots broke radio silence. It was not for any mission-critical purpose; they were arguing as to who had the rights to the pilot's Luger pistol, carried by all German pilots. It is hard to say to how much the actions of these two pilots were motivated by compassion and how much by a desire to obtain a prized war souvenir.

My final memory of war is traveling the Autobahn in a convoy and coming upon a group of tired, dirty and gaunt men. They were Allied POWs, whose German guards had abandoned their post, and now they were walking their way to freedom. As we passed slowly by them, the GIs in the jeeps and 6x6 trucks threw them whatever they had: cigarettes or candy bars or pieces of fruit. Watching these lethargic, half-starved men scramble and scurry in a kind of retarded slow-motion to pick up these meager tidbits, thrown to them as if they were a pack of hungry dogs, was heartbreaking.

Flying air reconnaissance was more than a two-man show. Our ground crews spent countless hours making sure our aircraft were airworthy.

GOING HOME

The war was nearly over. I was walking past the four-gun position
protecting our air strip in central Germany, when the distinctive,
crisply smooth sound of that Rolls Royce Merlin engine met my
ears. I waited for the plane to fly into the sight of my camera
lens—a young pilot, returning safely from a mission—heartened,
lifted in spirit, by his survival. There was no greater feeling, albeit
only momentary, in those days we all knew well.

DAZED AND CONFUSED

The surrender of Germany was drawing near, but V-E Day would offer little consolation for our squadron. Rumors were circulating that we were going to be transferred to the Pacific Theater once the fighting ceased, and we were not about to let our guard down quite yet.

Then somebody, my sergeant I think, came around saying, "They're cutting orders for everyone to go back to the States. They want everybody to go home before the unit gets clobbered by an order to go to the Pacific."

The sergeant was right. We were going home. I received my orders, put them in my pocket and proceeded to wander around for three, four, five days—I can't remember— in a kind of limbo.

I was relieved and thankful to be returning home and for the chance to see my family. But for how long? Was the war over for me? No one knew. It was like winning a pass to heaven that, at any moment, could be revoked in an instant by higher powers.

I packed all my gear, including my 2,000 coins collected during my European tenure, and boarded a plane for Paris. It was April in Paris, the last week of April to be exact, but I could not celebrate. I attended Les Folies Bergère, but left at intermission. I busied myself with taking pictures of the liberated city, including a young woman reading a book, which turned out to be, to my great discouragement, a pro-Communist tract, a kind of foreshadowing of the Cold War to come.

A young French woman in Paris. To my dismay, I discovered she was reading a pro-Communist tract.

OUTSIDE PARIS

My journey home began in this field just outside of Paris.

I was an unattached major in the United States Air Corps, billeted in a small village a few miles from the French capital. There were no missions to fly. No orders to obey. No squadron to command. I was waiting for my spot on a flight from Paris to London, and then on to the States. I was waiting to go home.

Often, with camera in hand, I would wander through the French countryside, exploring my new freedom.

For some reason, this ordinary scene caught my eye.

A single cow stands in the dappled shade of mid-day, chewing her cud in peace. And next to her, there for no apparent reason, what looks to be a cross. In the distance, a haystack, carved into a curious shape by the cows, reaching as high as they can to clutch the sweetest hay.

A French farmer riding a wagon comes along. He can't understand what I'm doing there. He stops for a moment to look me over, then turns left, heading away from me, looking back occasionally to see if I am still there. I snap the shutter.

It is hard for me to speak of this picture without emotion. Decades have passed and still, when I gaze upon this simple rustic scene, the realization that I had that day often overwhelms me.

Nobody is going to shoot me. I'm *safe*.

The release of tension which accompanied that simple thought was so visceral, so personal, that I did not talk about this picture with some members of my family for more than 60 years.

As the years have passed, I have gained a greater understanding of what I experienced that day outside of Paris. War had had its way with me. The stress of flying mission after mission, the sustained, continuous prospect of combat, and of death, had built up in me an ever present tension. For too long, a low-grade fear had burned in my gut and seeped into my bones. I had lived in this state of cautious vigilance for so long that I was not even aware of what a heavy burden I was carrying.

But on that day in the French countryside, the burden went away. To me, it was a thing of wonder that this French farmer was going about his business. For it meant that death and danger had been replaced by the ordinary and the uneventful. For two and a half years, I had not known if I was going to make it through the war alive. Now I knew I had. Like the people we had liberated, I was finally *safe*.

"JUST SEND ME HOME"

Eventually I flew from Paris to London and then to Stone, a redistribution point near Liverpool, where I awaited my final orders. On VE-Day, May 8, 1945, I found myself on a naval convoy traveling from England to America. Along the way, a German U-Boat surfaced, causing a brief alarm. Fortunately, the submariners had received word that the war was over, and now all they wanted to do was surrender. We stopped, took the German sailors aboard and hauled them all the way to Boston.

When we arrived, the Red Cross greeted us with pitchers of milk, wonderfully sweet, which I tasted for the first time since leaving the U.S. I traveled from Boston to Atlanta on a troop train so old and rickety that it seemed the wheels were square instead of round, with interminable delays as we waited on side tracks every time a regularly scheduled train needed to pass through.

Eventually I arrived at the troop redistribution center in Atlanta. I took a long 40-minute shower and lay down on a cot in the middle of the afternoon to take a nap. It all seemed unreal to me, being so close to home and so far away from the responsibilities of war. I felt unhinged.

In Atlanta I saw my sister Alice, who was working there with the Red Cross. She met me at the railway station as I was about to embark for Nashville.

The train arrived at Union Station in my hometown at 8:30 in the morning. There on the platform, my family awaited: mother, father, Auntie Margaret and Auntie Boo and more. But I was not there to greet them, thanks to my remarkable ability to fall asleep anywhere at any time. When everyone had departed the train, and no Joe had appeared, my father, an old railroad man, came aboard, found the one berth that was still closed, entered and awoke me, laughing and jovial. He only stayed a moment so I could wash briefly, put on my uniform and make myself acceptable.

When I saw them all, it was a joyous, but still reasonably restrained greeting. Mother cried. Auntie Boo kept peering over her glasses, looking at my medals and saying, "Little Joe, what are all these ribbons. What does this one mean? And this one?"

I felt no inclination to answer her, to explain that a bronze cluster was for five missions and a silver cluster was for 25 missions, and so on. It all sounded like Sunday School business to me, like having a discussion about the first chapter of Genesis after having just witnessed Creation itself.

Aunt Margaret hosted a wonderful party for me at Glen Leven. I was on a 30-day leave now, and in terms of military service, still not out of the woods completely. The war in the Pacific still raged on, and after my leave was up, I was sent to a redistribution center on the West Coast. I was stuck there for days until I finally asked a sergeant if I was going to be reassigned to the Pacific.

"How many points do you have," he asked.

"What points?" I asked naively.

"You're awarded points for overseas service, combat time and things like that," he said. "If you have enough, you can go home."

"How many do you need?" I asked.

"Seventy-five."

He took my 201 personnel file and off he went to calculate my destiny. Twenty minutes later, he came back with an odd expression on his face.

"Major, you have 192 points."

I paused. "So I can go home?"

"Right now, if you want," said the sergeant.

"What are my other options?" I asked.

The sergeant replied with a question of his own. "What would you like to do?"

I told him I was interested in going to the military photography school in Denver, where they were using the latest cameras and film technology. "Could you send me there directly?" I asked.

"No," said the sergeant. "I would have to reassign you to a squadron in the States."

And they could send me wherever they wanted?" I asked.

"Yep."

I didn't want any part of that. "Well then," I said. "Just send me home."

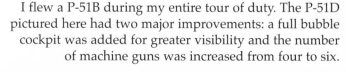

I flew a P-51B during my entire tour of duty. The P-51D pictured here had two major improvements: a full bubble cockpit was added for greater visibility and the number of machine guns was increased from four to six.

EPILOGUE

The camera used to take these pictures was a German-made Ikonta A that I bought at Dury's in downtown Nashville. The photographs would not have been possible without the assistance of Hugh Wingett of the old Burk & Co. in Nashville. He saved one or two rolls of film from his limited supply for my mother, who then mailed the precious rolls to me. I used Verachome film, 28 speed, with no light meter, and developed the film in my tent, pouring the developer and hypo into a small plastic tank, sponging them down and then noting the date and location in my logbook.

The original negatives of the nearly 600 images I took, as well as contact sheets and logbooks, are now part of the Nashville Room Collection at the Nashville Public Library.

When the war ended and I became a civilian, a new life emerged. After I decided not to attend photography school, my Aunt Mary directed me to visit Alden Smith, a Northwestern Mutual Agent who had recently returned from overseas to resume his career in the insurance business. Alden became my guide, and my inspiration, and set the pattern of behavior for a rewarding and purposeful career that, I hope, has been a valued service for many families for over 60 years.

The past was prologue to a remarkable journey. From my earliest days, I was blessed with a devoted family, a father who served as an artillery officer in World War I in France, and the undergirding strength of a wonderful mother. Then I received a solid education, followed by my service in a top notch Air Force unit in World War II. All of this background led to my experiences and survival—a providential path under God's direction.

A few highlights: my sudden revelation at the peaceful scene outside Paris, when I realized I had indeed survived—and a new life was ahead; the finding of a wife and the blessing of a family and a career.

Then, fifty years later, the remembrance of D-Day and World War II provided my wife and me the opportunity to rediscover the people of Normandy and other overseas friendships. This experience strengthened our belief that Almighty God was ever present, and that my survival was a part of His purpose for my future.

Now, as we see obvious changes measured against the past, I realize a different world is evolving in America itself, and in other countries —a decline in morality and purpose. This is our challenge.

God is in His heaven, and I hope many readers of this book will help to maintain what is right with the world.

Visiting the Normandy beachhead in May 1994, I befriended a group of French schoolchildren who were there on a field trip. Winning the war gave these children their freedom.

With my beloved wife Martha during our visit to England in May 1994.

JOE THOMPSON—SERVICE CHRONOLOGY

First Training Flight—Hicks Field	August 26, 1941
First Training Flight—Randolph Field	November 10, 1941
First Flight—Brooks Field	March 28, 1942
Transferred to 30th Observation Squadron	May 1942
Transferred to 109th Observation Squadron	July 1942
First flight in B-25	July 23, 1942
Sails from New York City for England	September 27, 1942
Arrives in Membury-Berkshire, England	October 16, 1942
Temporarily Transferred to 107th Squadron	November 16, 1942
Transferred to 109th Observation Squadron	April 22, 1943
First combat mission	September 9, 1943
Begins detached service with 66th RAF Squadron	October 2, 1943
Arrives in Normandy	July 4, 1944
Moves to Belgium	September 20, 1944
Arrives in Germany	March 24, 1945
Squadron moves to Kassel, Germany (R11)	April 7, 1945
Departs England for America	May 8, 1945
Arrives in Nashville on 30-day leave	June 9, 1945